Who's Got the Ball?

(and Other Nagging Questions About Team Life)

Coach Maureen O'Brien

Who's Got the Ball?

(AND OTHER NAGGING QUESTIONS ABOUT TEAM LIFE)

A Player's Guide for Work Teams

Jossey-Bass Publishers • San Francisco

Substantial discounts on bulk quantities of Jossey-Bass books are available to corporations, professional associations, and other organizations. For details and discount information, contact the special sales department at Jossey-Bass Inc., Publishers.

(415) 433-1740; Fax (800) 605-2665.

For sales outside the United States, please contact your local Paramount Publishing International office.

Manufactured in the United States of America on acid-free paper.

Library of Congress Cataloging-in-Publication Data

O'Brien, Maureen, date.
   Who's got the ball? : and other nagging questions about team life : a player's guide for work teams / Maureen O'Brien. — 1st ed.
      p.   cm. — (Jossey-Bass management series)
   ISBN 0-7879-0057-5
   1. Work groups. 2. Employee empowerment. I. Title. II. Series.
HD66.035   1995
658.3'128—dc20   94-23535

HB Printing 10 9 8 7 6 5 4 3 2 1   FIRST EDITION

Contents

PART THREE

PART FOUR

To my granddaughters—Tierney, Logan, Sara, Anja, Erin, and Casey. Writing this book was a dream of mine. I took my dream seriously and made it a goal. Never stop dreaming and always take your dreams seriously.

Preface

Today's employees are living through a major restructuring in the American workplace. The traditional hierarchical pyramid has not only been flattened; it has been reshaped into the corporate team circle. Eight out of every ten employees surveyed in a recent poll said that some form of teamwork existed in their workplace, and two-thirds said they actively participated in team activities (*The Quality Digest,* p. 10). Increasingly, organizations are removing management layers and charging employees with managing themselves and their functions as members of teams. Past organizational redesigns have required only minimal change, and many of them simply looked different on paper. Not this one!

To use a sports analogy, the game has changed from football to basketball. In football, the coach micro-manages. His primary focus is to develop the strategic game plan and then send in the tactical play-by-play decisions for the team to execute. The basketball coach, in marked contrast, macro-manages. He provides general direction; his primary focus is to develop positive chemistry among the players. He leaves much of the play-by-play decision making to the team. The difference is essentially one of empowerment. In football, the coach retains the power; in basketball, power is shared between the coach and the team players.

In the role of team leader, a manager must shift focus from decision making to team building. Employees, in their new role as team members, must shift focus from implementing directives to solving problems and making decisions as a team. Since this structure requires mutual cooperation and high levels of trust rather than unthinking obedience, team leaders and members must concentrate on developing effective relationships.

This role shift is confusing and frustrating to managers and employees alike. Because most team members and leaders have had little or no training in "teaming" concepts, they often try the old "throw it up against the wall and see if it sticks" approach. In too many cases it isn't sticking, and teams are struggling.

Despite their struggle, most employees are excited about the idea of being empowered and forming teams. They want this idea to work and they need help. My purpose in writing *Who's Got the Ball?* is to address that need. I want to help teams succeed. I know from my first-hand coaching experience why work teams are struggling and what they need to do to win. Very simply, I want to coach your team.

It seems I've been involved with teams all my life. After playing professional basketball, touring with the Harlem Globetrotters, and subsequently coaching in various athletic situations, I have spent the last twenty years in the field of organization and management development. As teaming became more widespread in the workplace, I found many opportunities to apply wisdom I had gained during my own athletic team days, and I developed a strategy called Scrimmage Training™ for coaching work teams.

During a sports scrimmage (practice game), the sports team plays as if it's in a real game. The major difference between a scrimmage and a real game is that during a scrimmage the coach can call unlimited time-outs to provide feedback to the team about its performance. This is action learning at its best. Seeing the enormous value of this coaching technique to my basketball teams, I decided to coach work teams the same way.

Scrimmage Training is live, on-the-job training that uses no role-playing, case studies, or simulations. I actually coach a team while they discuss and resolve real work issues during a two-day team meeting. I call time-out just like the basketball coach does during a scrimmage. This intimate coaching involvement has offered me a unique vantage point for observing the types of problems teams are encountering and for understanding the kinds of coaching interventions that help most.

That's what this book is about. You will be privy to the same coaching advice I give to my teams during Scrimmage Training. I will coach your team as up close and personal as the printed word allows. Sometimes I will present a concept that I feel is important for you to understand and suggest that you discuss it as a team. In other cases I will give you a technique and take you through specific steps to use it. When you finish reading this book you will understand this new game of teaming and you will have acquired the requisite skills to become a winning team.

Audience

My primary audience is working team members, but this book also has much to say to team leaders—who are, after all, members of the team, but who are also designated by senior management as accountable for managing and monitoring the team's performance. There are also a few important messages for senior management. The great strength of this book is that it is not theoretical. It offers hands-on advice gleaned from my own experiences with hundreds of teams. My recommendations are time tested; they are neither new nor experimental. If you learn best by discovering how teams have successfully grappled with situations similar to yours, this book is for you. *Who's Got the Ball?* is loaded with real-life anecdotes about teams. I'm sure as you read through the book you will find yourself saying, "That really sounds familiar."

My goal as your coach is to help your team win and to help you perform up to your full potential. I have been coaching organizational teams for fifteen years, and during that whole time I have been keeping notes from scrimmage sessions in my coaching file. You now hold that file in your hands. I can guarantee that these approaches will work for you.

Overview of the Contents

The book is organized into six Parts containing numerous freestanding Notes. Although I recommend reading the text in sequence, if you're experiencing a particular problem, by all means scan the Contents and move directly to the appropriate Note. Part One, Team Fundamentals, defines the basics shared by all high-performing teams. Part Two, Being a Valuable Team Member, focuses on your role and the inherent responsibilities you must accept to be an effective team member. The Notes in Part Three, Avoiding Common Team Problems, describe the common dysfunctions teams experience and offer advice on how you, as a responsible team member, can intervene to turn them around. Part Four, Running an Effective Team Meeting, provides tips for getting the most value out of your team meetings. In Part Five, Making Good Team Decisions and Putting Them into Play, you will gain insight into the concept of empowerment as it relates to decision making, and you will learn not only how to make good decisions but how to make sure you implement them. Part Six, Notes for Team Leaders, speaks directly to senior management and team leaders about the pivotal role they play in creating an organizational climate where teams can flourish.

Teaming is not a fad, and it's more than a theory or a technique. It's the new way of organizational life, and it's here to stay. Like those eastern European countries that have tasted democracy and want it to continue, organizations that have been successful with a team-based structure are not apt to turn back. I am convinced that this collection of team-coaching tips will work well for you and your teammates. If you find a tip you can use and someone asks where you got the idea, tell them it's from Coach O'Brien's file.

Acknowledgments

Writing this book has renewed my respect and admiration for authors. If their journey is anything like mine has been, it is a long and lonely one that requires patience, perseverance, and courage. In addition, I have learned that no matter how lonely the journey, one does not necessarily have to feel alone. I never did. Although my name is the only one that appears on the jacket of this book, it has not been a one-person show. I would like to share the credit with my invisible team who was with me at various steps along the way. Without their advice, support, and help I never would have made it across the finish line. My sincerest thanks go to the following:

All the teams I've been privileged to coach. I learned as much during our scrimmage sessions as they did. Without the richness of these experiences, this book would never have happened.

David Kimball, for his keen editorial eye, and for cheering me on each time I hit the wall in this writing marathon.

All my friends and colleagues, for their encouragement, and especially Barbara Mahon, Janet McConnell, and Alana M. Brahler, for muddling through the first drafts of the book. Their suggestions as a preliminary audience and their moral support were invaluable.

Joan Merillat, for her dedication to the project. Her speed was uncanny in transforming my handwritten, scribbled notes and cut-and-paste documents into formatted pages that resembled a book.

Marilyn Greenlaw, for her attention to detail in preparing the final manuscript for publication and for her unwavering personal and professional support.

Sarah Polster and Barbara Hill, my editors at Jossey-Bass, for continuously raising the bar and instilling in me the confidence I needed for the perfect jump. As a coach I know excellent coaching when I see it and that is what I received.

Lamar Adams, my dear friend, who believed in the value of this book from the very beginning and who nurtured me throughout the journey with his unconditional love and patience.

Myrtle Beach, South Carolina   Maureen O'Brien
February 1995

The Author

Coach Maureen O'Brien holds an M.A. degree in educational psychology and counseling from the University of Connecticut. Her extensive involvement in athletics, both as a touring professional basketball player with the Harlem Globetrotters and as a coach for various team sports, serves as the foundation for her unique Scrimmage Training approach to coaching work teams.

O'Brien is founder and president of OB Management Consultants, and she has worked in the field of management and organizational development for over twenty years. Her clients include a range of organizations—from blue-chip companies like IBM, General Electric, and Emerson to new companies attempting to get a foothold in the marketplace. She has specialized in team development for the past fifteen years. Before starting her own consulting business, she was manager of human resources development for Branson Ultrasonics Corporation and dean of students at the University of Connecticut, Waterbury.

PART 1

Team Fundamentals

Before you sign up for teaming, you'll want to know what is involved. Calling yourself a team does not make you a team and becoming one doesn't happen overnight. Forming a team takes time and hard work. The nine Notes in Part One identify the steps you must take in the start-up phase and discuss the developmental tasks you will face in your journey toward becoming a high-performing team.

In this Part, I will coach your team through the basics, get you started in the right direction, and provide the foundation shared by all winning teams.

Are You a Team?

Does this scene sound familiar? You and your colleagues have worked together as an effective department for many years when senior management announces that the organization will begin moving toward a team-based structure. Your department is instructed to form a team. You're not quite sure what this means because, as far as you're concerned, you already are a team. Three months later, you're even more confused. You are now calling yourselves a team, everyone is talking up this "teaming" stuff, and management seems to be expecting something different. But nothing has changed. You're still operating the same way—it's business as usual. This scenario is played out in many organizations on a daily basis for the simple reason that no one knows what a team is and, more important, what it takes to become one.

A team is a group of two or more people working together in an interdependent manner to achieve shared, common goals. Truly to be a team, you must satisfy the two operative requirements in the definition: "interdependence" and "common goals."

A group of people who work very well together might be described as demonstrating great teamwork and exceptional team spirit. They help each other out, come together in a crisis to douse the fires and keep the department running smoothly. Understandably, they think they are a team. They meet the requirement of "working together" with flying colors. There is a fundamental difference, however, between acting like a team and being a team.

Until a group establishes common, shared goals, something all members will be striving to achieve, it is not a team. It is a work group.

I can't emphasize strongly enough this major difference between a work group and a team.

Whether you are an existing work group or a group of people who have never worked together, you can't become a team until you establish your specific team goals. You must take this first step.

Call the group together and decide what you want to accomplish. Do you want to reduce rework by 15 percent, book five new customers per month, eliminate all the dead files, design a backup system?

As you can see, once you become a team with specific goals, you also have a scoreboard against which to measure your performance. With your scoreboard in place, I guarantee you'll see some changes: it won't be business as usual. As you reach each goal, you will have something to cheer about, something to celebrate.

Once you define your goals, give yourselves a standing ovation, pass out the cigars, treat yourselves to a leisurely lunch at a gourmet restaurant, or indulge in something equally pleasurable. You deserve it. You have just given birth to your team—one of the most challenging and difficult tasks you'll face.

What's Your Game?

I have never taken a sedative in my life. If I have trouble falling asleep, I start reading a technical article or book and within minutes, I'm dead to the world. That was my plan one night back in 1985 when I curled up with Robert Keidel's book *Game Plans: Sports Strategies for Business* (1985). That book was no sedative. The author's analogy of the teamwork processes and coaching strategies used by professional baseball, basketball, and football teams as these apply to business teams was so engrossing that I couldn't put the book down. I finished reading *Game Plans* at five in the morning and was on the phone to Bob about four hours later. For nine years now, I have been sharing his model with my teams. Thanks to Bob Keidel, I have been able to clear up confusion about how teams operate. Most people seem to think that a team is a team is a team. Not so; there are different kinds of teams.

The two elements that all teams share are common goals and the need for members to work together to achieve those goals. But based on the game they're playing and what it takes to win, there are and should be distinct differences in the way team members interact with and depend on each other, and the style of coaching required for team effectiveness. In other words, all teams are not alike. Your team may be organized and operate quite differently from other teams in your organization.

Even if you've never played baseball, basketball, or football, you're probably familiar with how each of these teams plays their game. Keep your team in mind as you read the following summary of Bob Keidel's thoughts on how these teams differ. You may be a pure team or a hybrid. For example, if the characteristics of your team's game closely resemble those of baseball, then you are what I would call a pure baseball-type team. On the other hand, although baseball may be your primary game, situations may arise that require you to play more like a basketball team. If that's the case, you are a hybrid baseball/basketball team.

The Baseball Team

Of the three types, the baseball team members are the least dependent on each other. Baseball is a very individualistic team sport. Players bat one at a time, and when the team takes the field to play defense, only two or three players come together to make a play. Although it rarely happens, the pitcher could conceivably strike out every batter he faces, a circumstance that would leave only the pitcher and catcher interacting for the entire game. The essential unit of the baseball team is the individual player. As Pete Rose once said, "Baseball is a team game, but nine men who reach their individual goals make a nice team" (Keidel, p. 6).

The primary focus of the baseball coach/manager is staffing: he decides who will be on the team and who will play in each game. In his recruiting efforts, he looks for superstars with the right technical skills to fill each of the nine positions. The more superstars on a baseball team the better. He also looks for players who can hit; you can never have too many hitters, particularly long ball hitters. Before the game, the coach decides the lineup as well as the batting order and the starting pitcher. Once the game begins, his role is limited. Even then his decisions have to do with staffing: who to put in as a designated hitter or runner and when to change the pitcher. Once he has the right players in the game, he expects them to excel in their specialized roles. As you can see, in baseball, the spotlight shines on individual players.

Baseball can best be described as a *player's game* and a game of *autonomy.*

The Basketball Team

At the other end of the spectrum, basketball teams have the highest level of player interdependence. All five players are in the game at the same time and each of them is fully involved in every play. Like the baseball team, each player has a designated position but, because the action of this game changes so quickly and unpredictably, the players must be very flexible, responding to each other in a spontaneous and reciprocally cooperative manner. Each player must assume a variety of roles and be ready to support the team on a split second's notice. As Bill Russell said, "In each split second, a basketball game changes as fast as ten rapidly moving objects can create new angles and positions on the floor. Your game plan may be wiped out by what happens in the first minute of play. Each player has to predict where a pattern of action will lead, and then act to change that pattern to the advantage of his team. Teams that can do this under the greatest pressure will win most of the time" (Keidel, p. 55).

The name of the game is to put the ball through the hoop more often than the opposing team does. Unlike baseball, where too much hitting is never a problem, too much shooting *can* be a problem. If one player is intent on being the superstar and shoots the ball every time he gets it, the team will very likely lose the game. The best basketball teams have a great passing game. Players unselfishly share the ball in an effort to set up a teammate for the easy shot. This is not to say that basketball teams don't have their superstars. Michael Jordan and Magic Johnson were certainly superstars for their respective teams but if you look at the statistics, they were both unselfish players and are as well known for assists (setting up the good play) as they are for scoring.

The basketball team coach concentrates on process—the flow of the game and how the players on the court are interacting with each other. His primary focus is to develop the team's ability to coordinate and manage themselves. There are limited time-outs during the game and the coach's on-line influence is minimal. The team must make its own decisions and make them very quickly. Most important, the coach must create a positive chemistry among team players. Where the strength of a baseball team comes from individual players' technical competence, the basketball team's major asset is strong, trusting, interpersonal relationships among the players and between the players and the coach. Under Red Auerbach, the Boston Celtics won a phenomenal nine championships in a ten-season run. While talking about his philosophy of trading players, he said, "To me the best trade is no trade. Even if you can get a player who's better than your guy, it's not always a good deal. The new guy might rub your players the wrong way, and that's a killer in this game" (Keidel, p. 99). In basketball, the entire team is showcased; the spotlight does not shine on any individual player. It is definitely a *team* game and a game of *cooperation*.

The Football Team

Like the basketball team members, football players are highly dependent on each other. This is a different kind of interdependence, however, and the two teams operate quite differently. Where the interaction of basketball players is spontaneous and voluntary, teamwork in football can best be described as sequential and prescribed. The football team is much like a machine. When George Allen was head coach of the Washington Redskins, he described the football team this way: "A football team is made up of parts. If one part doesn't work, one player pulling against you and not doing his job, the whole machine fails" (Keidel, p. 8). This is most evident when a player in the offensive line fails to perform his scripted part of the play. When this happens it puts the quarterback and the running backs in jeopardy. The quarterback must now make unexpected adjustments and may not be able to get the pass off. He may even get sacked. And if he has been able to hand off to the running backs, there probably are no holes open through which they can run the ball. This failure of the lineman can spell the difference between the team's gaining a first down and retaining possession of the ball, which is what it takes to win football games, or having to punt and turn the ball over to the opponents.

The football team is also structured into platoons: offense, defense, and transition and smaller special teams for kickoff, punt, or field goal situations. A high level of interaction and coordination is required within each of these platoons but not necessarily between or among them. The defensive team sits on the bench while the offensive team does battle on the field and vice versa. Special teams assemble and interact only when the game situation calls for it. The essential unit of the football team is the *platoon*.

The football coach is the strategic planner and commander in chief. He decides in advance which plays and formations will work best against the opposing team. He reviews his game plans with the team, runs the players through the necessary drills during practice sessions, and expects them to work his plan. The quarterback, as leader of the offensive team on the field, is a surrogate coach. He relays the coach's play to the team in the huddle but can call an audible on the line of scrimmage, changing the original scripted play if he notices the opponents setting up in a formation different from what was expected. Unlike basketball players who are in control of their game and responsible for making team decisions, football players, except for the quarterback, make no decisions. The coach is in control; he calls the plays and the team's responsibility is to execute them. Jimmy Johnson, former coach of the superbowl-winning Dallas Cowboys, is well known for his confrontational style of coaching. Commenting on his reputation, he once said, "You don't shy away from confrontations in the job, or the players will walk all over you. I want to jump in because I want to be in control. I want to be in control because I want to win. And in order to win you've got to have a guy solidly in control of the team. . . . Some of my players may hate my guts, but either way I'll be in control and we will win. The players understand that" (King, p. 5). Football is very much a *coach's game* and a game of *control*. In fact, the coach is so much in the limelight that he gets the credit if the team has a winning season and he may well be out of a job if the team performs poorly.

What game is your team playing? If your success depends on individual technical expertise (superstars in each position), and the need for teamwork is infrequent and situational, then baseball is your game. It is critical that you be staffed appropriately with the right players in the right position at the right time. Some of the baseball teams I've coached include sales teams, administrative support teams, university faculty teams, and customer service teams. In their start-up phase, members often have a difficult time envisioning themselves as a team. Since their allegiance has been to their client and because management, up to this time, has focused solely on individual performance, the players do not readily recognize the common goals that bind them as a team. Once they begin to look at the larger organizational goals and how they can contribute to them collectively, their team image becomes clear. I find that members of baseball-type teams tend to miss the sense of belonging and cohesiveness that come with playing basketball. I always recommend that they become a hybrid team— baseball/basketball—by establishing a few basketball-type goals that require all players to work together. Recently I coached a sales team that did just that. Each member removed his sales district cap and the entire team collaborated on designing a new sales reporting process.

If you are the leader of a baseball team and your style is more like that of a football coach, you will need to make some major adjustments. Home run hitters know how to hit the ball. You will lose key players and frustrate your team if you don't allow them to get up to bat and do what they already know how to do.

If your team's competitive edge is flexibility and the ability to respond to change and create change quickly, basketball has to be your game. Since all members are so highly dependent on each other, it is critical that you work at developing a high level of cohesiveness and trust and learn how to work together in a cooperative manner. You must be especially willing to ask for help and to give help voluntarily. You must monitor your team process continuously and self-correct when the flow of the game is preventing you from winning. If you are a cross-functional team, the more you can learn about each other's functional responsibilities, the more sensitive you will be to your teammates' problems. Some of the strongest basketball teams I've known have gone beyond learning about their teammates' functions—they have actually cross-trained each other so they can, in effect, perform each other's functions. Your resources are team resources so you must be willing to share them for the benefit of the team.

If you are leading a basketball team and your natural style is more like that of the baseball coach, you will have to get more involved with the team. It's not a hands-off job; you must be the catalyst for creating positive chemistry and you must teach the team how to manage their own game. One of the most dramatic disconnects I've seen between leadership style and team is the football-oriented coach leading a basketball team. I call it the Bobby Knight disconnect. As coach of the Indiana University basketball team, Bobby seems to have an inordinate need to be in control of his team. I can't argue with his winning records but my own personal opinion is that his coaching philosophy is more suited to football. It may work on occasion in college basketball where the season is short and the players are young and impressionistic, but I can guarantee it doesn't work for organizational work teams.

If your work must be tightly controlled to avoid the risk of failure and the steps in your work process are sequential, your game is football. Manufacturing teams using mass production and airline teams responsible for the safe takeoff and landing of aircraft are typically organized and coached in the football mode. As a frequent flyer, I am delighted to know that the leader of the airline team has a specific plan in mind and that the team members are mandated to execute the plan.

Pure football-type teams are becoming more and more rare in the workplace of the 1990s. Most organizations that have evolved to a team-based structure have done so because the top-down hierarchical control of football management doesn't work in today's fast-paced, ever-changing business environment. The employees who do the work know best how to do it and therefore should be empowered to make operational decisions. That is accomplished by individual players in the baseball orientation and by the team in the basketball orientation; however, there is always a need for football coaching no matter what type of team you are. When safety, corporate policy, and governmental restraints are part of the game, the team leader must act as the football coach and make command decisions.

Whether you are an established team or are just forming your unit you will find it worthwhile to determine what game you are playing. Knowing your game will tell you the teamwork strategies and the coaching skills you need to come out on top. Share this Note with your teammates and set this topic—"What's our game?"—as an agenda item for discussion at a team meeting. You might want to use the "What's Your Game?" questionnaire as a springboard for your team discussion by either filling it out together or by having each member fill it out before you meet.

WHAT'S YOUR GAME?

Now that you have a general sense of how baseball, basketball, and
football teams play their game, let's see which sport your game most re-
sembles. In other words, what's your game? Respond to the nine team
descriptions below by selecting the *one* statement (a), (b), or (c), that *best*
describes your team, in *most situations.*

1. When we have a big win, it's primarily a result of
   a. Superstar performance by one or more individual members
   b. The team's precise execution of a detailed plan
   c. The team's willingness to be flexible and its ability to
      innovate
2. For the most part, when we experience problems and issues,
   a. Our leader brings them to the attention of the team and we fix
      them
   b. Our leader assigns the problem to one or two players to fix
   c. Our leader tells us how to fix it
3. Our work interfaces can best be described this way:
   a. Members perform specific functions and hand off work in a
      systematic, sequential manner
   b. Members of the whole team are highly dependent on each
      other and interact frequently
   c. Members are fairly autonomous; everyone tends to do his or
      her own thing
4. We place a high value on
   a. Recruiting the best and the brightest players
   b. Having established procedures to avoid unnecessary risks
   c. Responding quickly to change in a cooperative and collabora-
      tive manner
5. Our members tend to identify with and have a sense of loyalty to
   a. The team itself
   b. Their profession and the particular industry or client they serve
   c. Their particular work function (for example, marketing, engi-
      neering, finance, manufacturing)

6. Our team leader's style can best be described as
   a. Hands-on and autocratic—a strategic planner who calls the shots
   b. Hand in hand and participative—a player/coach
   c. Hands-off—behind the scenes tactician
7. The nature of our game is
   a. Slow-paced and somewhat unpredictable
   b. Moderately paced and predictable
   c. Fast-paced and ever-changing
8. Our teamwork can best be described as
   a. Spontaneous
   b. Situational
   c. Preplanned
9. When one member of our team fails to fulfill his or her role responsibilities, the impact on other team members' performance is
   a. Significant; it can actually cause everyone to fail
   b. Moderate, but usually we can make some adjustments and get everyone back on track
   c. Minimal; other team members can still perform well

If the pattern of your responses for the nine statements was A B C A B C A B C, you are clearly playing baseball. If your pattern looks like B C A B C A B C A, you resemble more a football team. And if you responded C A B C A B C A B, it looks like basketball is your game.

	BASEBALL	*FOOTBALL*	*BASKETBALL*
1.	A	B	C
2.	B	C	A
3.	C	A	B
4.	A	B	C
5.	B	C	A
6.	C	A	B
7.	A	B	C
8.	B	C	A
9.	C	A	B

What's Your Noble Purpose?

What is your team's raison d'être? Why do you exist? What significant contribution does your team make to the organization, the community, society, the world? This is the first question I pose to teams during their "scrimmage" game. My goal is to have teams think about and verbalize not just *what* they do, but *why* they do it and therefore, why it is critical that they do it well. Ultimately, I want them to understand their *noble purpose.*

The immediate response of most people to this question usually sounds like "getting to know you" cocktail party banter. "We keep records"; "We're the Shipping Team; we get the product out." What have I learned? I now know the team's title and the function they perform. I also know that the team has no sense of their importance. It's not unusual for teams, or for that matter individuals, to lack this awareness. But without it, people are less likely to be excited about their jobs or committed to excellence.

For your team to be energized and motivated toward superior performance, you must elevate your thinking beyond title and function and own your noble purpose.

A favorite old saw speaks to the need for such a purpose:

Three bricklayers were busy at their trade at the same site. A passerby approached the first and asked what he was doing. The workman responded, "I'm laying bricks." To the second workman he posed the same question and was told, "I'm building a wall." When asked the same question, the third bricklayer replied, "I'm building a magnificent cathedral so people from all over the world may come and experience serenity, be at peace, and worship their God."

Of these, the third bricklayer articulated *noble purpose.* He had moved beyond title and task to purpose. He was inspired and invigorated because he understood that his work was important and that he was making a significant contribution.

Noble purpose not only energizes teams; it also provides focus and influences how the team approaches their work. Recently I was coaching a team who called themselves the "Employee Functions Team." They were working in an organization that had merged two divisions with distinctly different cultures and values. The team had already developed their mission statement, which read: "We provide fun activities for employees in our organization."

I pointed out to them that their statement clearly described what they did and whom they did it for. All they had to do now was to take it to another level and answer this question: Why are we providing fun activities? What are we trying to accomplish? What significant contribution will we make to the organization? Their final mission statement was a triumph in noble purpose clarity. It read: "We create harmony and unity among employees by providing fun, social activities."

Once the Employee Functions Team included their noble purpose in their mission statement, they had an entirely new focus. They now felt they were doing something important. They had become one pumped-up, turned-on team!

They were still planning fun activities, but now they made sure that their functions brought the employees from the two divisions together, stimulated their getting to know and enjoy one another, and helped to heal the hard feelings that the merger had wrought. In so doing they had a major role in removing barriers and strengthening the organization.

If you haven't yet crafted a formal mission statement, I encourage you to do so. It should clearly explain your team's function (what you do) and your team's noble purpose (why you do it, the impact you have). Noble purpose is the energizing piece of your mission statement; it's what makes your team feel important. If you have a mission statement that does not include your noble purpose, recharge your battery. Take some time off from the work you do and get a clear focus on *why* you do it.

Two steps will help you define your noble purpose:

1. Using the brainstorming technique, complete the following sentences:

   Our team is important because we _____
   If it weren't for us, _____

2. Read the sentences you've created aloud and respond to this statement:

   Big deal! Why is that so important?

This exercise will elevate your thinking even further and by the time you have completed it, you will more than likely have arrived at your noble purpose. You may have to ask "Why is that so important?" several times before you get it precisely right.

For example, "If it weren't for us, our employees would be unaware of and confused about their benefits." Why is that so important? "The time employees spend researching their benefits is time spent away from work so we are enhancing our employees' productivity."

Are You Winning?

Watch any team athletic event, no matter the sport, and the one thing you will always see is a scoreboard. I can't imagine a team playing without one, can you? After all, they're playing to win and the only way they can tell if they've won is to keep score.

And yet, I have coached work teams who have no idea whether they're winning or losing. They know they're working hard but they haven't a clue what they're working toward. When I ask them what their major goals are for the next six to twelve months, some teams say, "We want to become a great team." This response always reminds me of a scene from the play *The Search for Signs of Intelligent Life in the Universe,* starring Lily Tomlin. Chrissy, feeling down and out because she's been unable to hold down a job and keeps getting rejected in job interviews, says to her friend, "All my life I've always wanted to be somebody, but I see now I should have been more specific." It's a wonderfully funny and poignant line and speaks to the kind of insight your team should have. Specifically, how will you know you are great? Where is your scoreboard?

Then there are those teams whose stated goals are to improve customer service, increase productivity, reduce costs. These teams are at least starting to focus; they know the critical areas demanding their attention but they have yet to put a stake in the ground. Still, no scoreboard.

How do you create your team scoreboard? You can begin by answering a simple question: How will we know we've been successful? How will others know? If you say you want to improve customer service, what do you want to see? Is it fewer complaints from customers? Is it more positive ratings on your customer service survey? Is it quicker response time to customer problems? You're almost there when you answer these questions, but you still won't know if you're winning until you have added yet more specificity. You need some numbers, some quantifiable way to measure your success.

The final step to ensuring goal clarity and creating a scoreboard that will be visible to you and to your fans is to answer these two questions: *How* will we measure our success? *When* do we want to achieve this goal? Answer these questions and you have a scoreboard that might look like this:

- Reduce the number of customer complaints by 20 percent by third quarter of 1995.

- Reduce turnaround time from 5 days to 3 days by August 1, 1995.

- Increase positive ratings on Customer Satisfaction Survey by 25 percent by January 1996.

- Reduce the number of times the customer's telephone call is put on hold by 50 percent by October 1995.

Staying focused on your goals is key to winning. Maintain your focus by posting your scoreboard in a central location, visible to all team members and others in the organization. And don't forget to keep your eye on the game clock. You've set a completion date for each goal so the clock is running. Call periodic time-outs to assess your progress against your end goal. You may need a brief pep rally or a change in strategy— or you may be pleasantly surprised to find that you are right on track.

Like sports teams, you can now play to win. May you have many victories, now that you know how to keep score!

Human Doings
Versus Human Beings

If your team is currently operating at high levels of productivity but you and other team members would give anything to cancel your membership, you've probably become a team of human doings at the expense of being human beings. What you are experiencing is an imbalance between satisfying the *task* needs and satisfying the *relationship* needs of your team. If this imbalance continues, your team is headed for trouble; you can expect productivity to plummet in the near future. You need to refocus. Continue to keep your eye on the work but start to pay equal attention to team members' feelings and needs.

There are two sides to the team effectiveness equation: task and relationship. To become a high-performing team, you must be proficient at both. Let me explain:

The task side concerns productivity or getting the job done. Your team has tasks to be completed and goals to achieve; after all, that is why you formed your team. To be effective on the task side, you need to be *human doings*. Most teams I've coached excel at human doing. They're good at planning, organizing, scheduling, and completing the work that needs to be done. As they've told me, "We can't afford to be weak on the task side. There's so much to do; we're living in a world of doing more with less."

The relationship side of the equation has to do with cohesiveness—pulling together as a team and developing positive relationships. Your team has members who have feelings; to be productive, they need to feel respected, valued, included, empowered, and excited about being a member of the team. To satisfy these needs, you must invite ideas and opinions, actively listen to one another, offer assistance, share information, encourage participation, and praise outstanding performance. In other words, you need to be effective *human beings*. This side of the equation is often overlooked by teams.

As I work with teams and point out the need for task and relationship balance, their initial response is, "We don't have time for this 'touchy, feely' stuff. We're not being measured on how our teammates feel; it's what we get done that counts."

I truly understand the need for results. We all need to remember, however, that when human beings don't feel valued, accepted, and respected, over time they will lose their motivation to produce.

All high-performing teams have the right stuff—and it's not "touchy, feely"; it's "tasky, feely." That's a balance of human doing and human being. The Notes in the following Parts provide more detailed information and techniques you can use to strike that balance.

It's Just a Stage

Teams have a life cycle, punctuated with four predictable stages of growth that are comparable to those of human development. Bruce Tuckman (1965) named these stages *forming, storming, norming,* and *performing.*

During the *forming* stage, your team is born and like the young child, its primary need is to establish a unique identity. Once your team defines who it is and why it exists, the team will move to the *storming* stage, which can be likened to adolescence. It's not a fun place to be. Like the teenager, your team will struggle with feelings of disillusionment, frustration, and at times even hopelessness.

But remember, you're just going through a stage. This too shall pass, and when it does your team will enter the *norming* stage. At this point you will breathe a huge sigh of relief as you begin to feel the same sense of burgeoning maturity, stability, and productivity that the young adult feels. The world is your oyster now. You begin to feel a sense of worth; you just need to sort out priorities, put some plans together, and go after what you want.

The next stage is what you've been striving for all along. You've reached the pinnacle of success—the *performing* stage. Like the fully mature adult, you take full responsibility for who you are, manage your own affairs, and feel that you're in control of your destiny. You feel confident, are highly productive, and at the same time experience a true harmony. When you reach the performing stage you'll know it. It's not an easy task to grow into your full potential. Yours has been a courageous journey.

Your team will experience similar dynamics during each stage. This evolution is not only predictable, it's healthy. Like any living, growing organism, your team will meet the challenges of each stage and bridge these stages by tending to specific developmental tasks. What follows is a synopsis of these developmental tasks and one team member's description of what each stage actually felt like.

The Forming Stage

In this stage you get organized. Your tasks are to establish your mission, your team goals, your member roles and responsibilities, your team ground rules, and the structure for your team meetings. One team member articulated his thoughts about this phase as follows:

> We were all fairly eager to form our team even though we weren't quite sure what teaming was about. All the team members seemed to be on their best behavior—you know, very polite and respectful. But you could sense that communication was guarded. Members never shared what they were feeling. I was confused and anxious and I'm sure others were as well, but nobody said anything about it. There also weren't any conflicts at this point, which was kind of nice. We were all trying to figure things out like, Why are we forming a team? What's my role on the team going to be? How is being a team going to be different? How are we going to work together? What's our leader going to be like? Will he act the same as he did when he was our manager? Are we really going to make more decisions than we did before? What is management expecting from us? There seemed to be more questions than there were answers.
>
> We knew we needed structure but we didn't know how to get it. We looked to our leader for direction—actually, we were very dependent on him. He was great. He explained all the tasks we needed to do and

then guided us through each one of them. We agreed on some ground rules, crafted a mission statement, and established specific team goals. Then we looked at specific tasks that needed to be done and did a skills inventory to see who could do what so we could define each of our roles and responsibilities. Our leader set some general guidelines about which decisions he felt we should make at this point.

Our leader also conducted some team-building exercises, which turned out to be a really fun way for us to get to know one another on a personal level. These forming tasks took a fair amount of time so our productivity was somewhat low but I would say our morale was high. We had the structure in place and were raring to go.

The Storming Stage

In this stage you learn how to work together. Your primary tasks are to develop teamwork behaviors that build trusting relationships, enhance member participation, inclusion, and involvement, create feelings of personal empowerment, and facilitate conflict resolution. Check out your ground rules during this stage. Are team members living by them or are they just words on paper? Review your goals and roles to clarify organizational issues that may remain from the forming stage. About this phase, the team member commented:

We seemed to lose our etiquette skills during this stage as we went from being on our best behavior to being on our worst. It seemed like everyone was vying for the star position. If you've ever seen a basketball team whose players are ball hungry and want to shoot all the time instead of setting up a play, that's what we were like.

The ground rules we had agreed to went down the tubes. If any rule was in effect it was, "Agree to disagree with everything and everyone and when possible, throw in a little finger-pointing." Gradually factions developed and we became splintered into these little sub-groups. Then, you could almost predict who was going to support whose ideas and who was going to kill whose ideas. Conflicts began to brew but about the only thing anyone did about them was talk about them behind everyone's back. It was very frustrating for everyone. Some of us were angry because we had thought teaming was going to be a great thing; we felt we had been duped and were terribly disillusioned. We were particularly angry with our leader. All of these great plans that he had helped us with had looked great on paper but the reality of what we were working on, who was doing what, and how we were working together was so different. Many of us had misgivings; there were times we were ready to throw in the towel.

Eventually we revisited our goals and roles and made some minor changes that seemed to clear things up. Our team leader was a great coach and role model. He lived by the ground rules we had established and continuously gave us feedback when we failed to follow them, pointing out how ignoring the rules was affecting our performance. Slowly we began to get our act together; the factions all but disappeared as members began to bond with each other. I think the biggest improvement came when we stopped all the grandstanding. We began to listen to each other, build on each other's ideas, and give power to each other by showing a willingness to be influenced. To go back to my basketball analogy, we began to pass the ball around and set each other up for good shots.

Despite the antagonistic attitude that members had displayed toward our leader, he never stopped supporting us throughout this stage. He kept saying, "Hang in there; we'll make it if we just keep working at it." Without his encouragement, I'm not sure we would have grown out of this ugly stage. It was obvious we were still very dependent on him, which I think is one of the things that disturbed us so. We thought we should have been able to function on our own.

The Norming Stage

In this stage you heighten focus on your team's productivity and cohesiveness. Your primary task is to monitor team performance by evaluating your processes. The major questions during this stage are, "How are we doing? Are we achieving our goals? Do members feel good about being a part of this team?" You've made a quantum leap from the storming stage to the norming stage and it feels pretty darn good. You're beginning to feel like winners but you won't take first place unless you stay focused and as a team accept responsibility for self-correcting. The shift in the members' self-confidence is evident from the team member's remarks:

We felt like we had been launched. Finally we were a team and were very proud of the quantum leap forward we were making in our productivity and in the way we supported each other. Sometimes it was hard to believe how far we had come. Teaming was exciting again and we were enjoying a newfound serenity. In the beginning of this stage, there were very few conflicts. Everyone seemed to be enjoying the peace and was making every effort to avoid going back to our fighting days.

Our leader kept encouraging us to coach ourselves. We became increasingly introspective and began to call our own "time-outs" when a member broke a ground rule or when we thought we could improve our process. I guess you could say we were in a continuous improvement mode. Also, for the first time I'd have to say we began to genuinely trust each other and our leader. As this trust increased, I noticed a marked difference in how members communicated with each other. It was more authentic; people began to say what was on their minds. We began to have conflicts again, but now we were better equipped to resolve them.

I think our leader trusted us from day one but now it was more evident as he began to transfer more and more decisions and responsibilities to us. There was no doubt that we were less dependent on him and that felt awfully good. We really began to focus on our goals during this stage and put together plans to achieve them. I think we sensed that there was nothing we couldn't tackle. We also knew we could get even better.

The Performing Stage

Here's when you give each other a standing ovation. You are a winning, championship team! It's a great feeling and you've earned the right to celebrate. It's equally important that you keep the momentum going, so don't rest on your laurels. Championship teams repeat their victories by emphasizing the best practices they have developed along the way.

We knew we were a championship team. Our leader told us in so many ways but mostly by moving farther and farther out of the picture. He was still there when we needed him—and we did at times— but at this point we felt very much empowered. We decided how to resolve productivity issues, influenced hiring decisions, monitored our own performance, and even designed and conducted our own peer performance reviews. Seems we were also privy to more and more information about the business. No question about it, we played a major part in the success of the business. It was great knowing we had such an impact.

We really cared about each other, not just as it related to work but from a personal perspective. The camaraderie and team spirit was wonderful. We had all kinds of conflicts but we worked hard to resolve them immediately and we usually did. We were committed to giving each other feedback, both positive and negative, on a regular basis. I don't know of many teams that had the confidence we did.

We had become a team of many leaders, all of us feeling an equal responsibility for the team's success. Although the organization and our leader recognized our achievements, there was an internal satisfaction that could not be denied. One of the important things we learned during this stage was to celebrate our victories.

What Does a High-Performing Team Look Like?

I'm often asked, "How will we know when we've become a high-performing team?" In actuality, you never really become one, just like you never become a fully mature adult. You are always in the process of becoming; it is a journey.

I realize that's not a very definitive answer. Most teams want to chart their growth, and to do this, they need ways to measure it. One approach is to look at the characteristics that high-performing teams share and to measure your growth within these features. These characteristics are listed and discussed below so that you can compare your team's performance to them.

- *Always keep score.* Excellent teams are clear about what they are trying to achieve and about what roles team members must play in order to win. In other words, they have both goal clarity and role clarity. They constantly revisit their goals to make sure they are maintaining focus. Because they have such a specific scoreboard they know when they've won. They don't allow themselves to get complacent, but they do celebrate their victories.

- *Feel important.* High-performing teams are committed to achieving their goals and are motivated toward excellence because they understand the significant contribution they make. They have a clear sense of their noble purpose.

- *Have balance.* Equally concerned about quality of work and quality of life, outstanding teams are dedicated to doing the job well and treating all members with respect. They strive for high levels of productivity and cohesiveness and are successful in both areas.

- *Self-correct.* High-performing teams are willing to admit mistakes when things go wrong and are constantly looking for ways to improve. They welcome the opportunity to change their processes and procedures if doing so makes them more productive.

- *Encourage diversity.* These teams guard against "groupthink" (going along with the majority view) by encouraging members to express their honest opinions. Because they place such a high value on diverse opinions and ideas, they experience plenty of conflict. They work toward resolving conflicts immediately, realizing that doing so will make them a stronger team.

- *Share leadership and power.* Team members welcome outside influence; they listen actively and consider other members' ideas. Their philosophy is, "It's a good idea to explore all ideas." Consensus is their preferred decision-making mode when they are making major team decisions. The team is minimally dependent on the designated leader. All members are considered leaders of the team.

- *Work at developing trust among team members.* Members' behavior engenders rather than erodes trust. When personality conflicts surface, they deal with them directly, using constructive feedback as a vehicle.

- *Encourage full participation.* In a high-performing team, all members are expected to contribute from the point of idea

RATING SCALE FOR TEAM PERFORMANCE

Characteristics of High-Performing Teams	Low Level of	Medium Level of	High Level of
Goal Clarity			X
Role Clarity			X
Commitment to Excellence			X
Feelings of Importance (Clarity of Noble Purpose)			X
Balance—Task and Relationship			X
Flexibility—Willingness to Change			X
Candid/Open Communication			X
Willingness to Confront and Resolve Conflict			X
Shared Leadership			X
Receptivity to Members' Ideas			X
Trusting Relationships			X
Participation and Involvement			X
Support to Members— Offering Encouragement and Praise			X
Shared Accountability and Responsibility			X
Productivity			X
Cohesiveness			X

creation straight through to the implementation of decisions. Team members generate energy by providing positive feedback to each other. They share full responsibility and accountability for all successes and failures.

The characteristics discussed above have been converted into the "Rating Scale for Team Performance." This simple rating scale can serve as a kind of yardstick to help your team evaluate its growth. Ask all members to rate the team on the sixteen measures. Where does your team's performance fit in? If you're in the forming or storming stage, don't expect your profile to look like this one. It takes time and hard work to become a high-performing team. Don't get discouraged either—just focus in on those characteristics you still need to develop.

Your Team Is One Player in a Bigger Game

I have seen work teams become so self-centered that they were actually a destructive force within their organization. In their striving for high performance, they focused solely on their own development, goals, strategies, and processes, and they began unconsciously to compete with other teams in the organization. They wanted management to see them as a "stand-out" team and in the process lost sight of their real goal, which was to make their organization a winner in the marketplace.

Competition is great, but it's important to get your competitive juices flowing in the right direction. Who is your competition? Is it a small shop down the street or are you playing in the International Business League? If you don't know who your organization is competing against, find out. Then take a look at how your team, working together with other teams, can beat them. Your organization is really one big team, made up of smaller, interdependent teams. If you want to win, it is critical that your smaller teams work together collaboratively.

To ensure that this is happening, examine how your team interacts with the rest of the organization. Here is a list of questions to help you get started. If you answer "No" or "I don't know" to any of them, corrective action is indicated. If you answer "Yes" to all, keep up the good work!

- Are you sure there is no duplication of effort occurring between your team and other teams?

- When you are planning or designing a new approach, system, or process, do you invite those teams or people who will be affected to the planning meetings?

- When your team makes decisions, do you consider the impact on other teams?

- When your team is caught up with its workload, do you offer help to other teams?

- When there is a work-related problem with another team, do you refrain from finger-pointing and instead get together with that team to solve the problem?

- Do you publicly thank those teams who have helped you through their outstanding performance?

- Do you share with other teams your best practices—those techniques and procedures that work particularly well for you?

All High-Performing Teams Have Ground Rules

Bruce is the most successful team leader I've ever known. Two years ago, he accepted an assignment to lead one team. Today he is leading five, all of which are minimally dependent on him. In other words, he has brought them all to the high-performing stage. I asked him, "If you could give only one tip to teams, what would it be?" "That's a no brainer," he answered. "Ground rules—they're a team's guiding light." Elaborating on this, he said:

> Nothing helps a team so much. Each of my teams has different ones, of course, because they establish the rules for themselves. They're not my ground rules and they have nothing to do with company rules or policy. They are the local rules of play and they always have to do with behavior. My teams constantly look at member behavior and decide which behaviors work and which ones get in the way. Then they come up with team ground rules that specifically prohibit the hindering behavior and encourage the helpful behavior. The team also agrees that every member is responsible for letting a team member know when he or she is not abiding by the ground rules. That's what makes the rules come alive. Team members are committed to them and willing to monitor themselves against them. That would be my one tip. Have your team establish its ground rules.

Team ground rules are agreements among team members about the group's standard of behavior. They are established by the team and for the team, and they cover every kind of situation a team can think of: meetings, problem solving, decision making, conflict resolution, communication, backups, and leadership, to name just a few.

Teams start to establish ground rules quite naturally during their norming stage. At this point in their development, they've usually been working together for a while and have developed trust enough to start talking candidly about behavior that is holding them back. I remember in one such team discussion, a member said, "You know, it's really hurting us when members come late to meetings. We end up having to review everything to bring the tardy member up to date. It's a total waste of time. Besides, it bothers me personally; it's disrespectful to the rest of us who are on time."

At the conclusion of their discussion, this team had established a ground rule, unwritten but clearly understood by all: everyone was expected to arrive on time for team meetings.

The same team began to realize that it was not following through on team decisions promptly. The members agreed that every time a decision was made they would immediately determine the action items necessary to implement it. They were so diligent about practicing this ground rule that it became one of their good habits. Any time they make a decision now, a member always asks, "What do we need to do to make this happen? Who is going to do it? When will they have it completed?" Ground rules are like that; in time they become good habits.

I've seen many teams dramatically improve their performance simply by identifying their dysfunctional behaviors and establishing ground rules to prohibit them. But why wait until you're dysfunctional? Start-up teams reap the same benefits from ground rules as do veteran teams. When I work with start-up teams, I insist that they agree on some ground rules before they take on other tasks—even before they define their team goals. If yours is a start-up team, I encourage you to do the same. You don't have to share a history of working together to know which behaviors will help and which might hurt your team's performance.

Here are a few hints to help you establish your ground rules and some tips for making them work for you:

1. *Make sure your ground rules are behaviorally defined;* it's the only way you can tell whether members are living by them. Behavior is observable. It's action you can see and hear and that everyone would objectively agree is happening. Ground rules like "Have a positive attitude," or "Show respect for all members" sound good but they're useless. They don't work because they are not behavior-specific. Positive attitude and respect are not behaviors; they are *attributes* of behavior. You can't see respect nor can you hear it, and we may not all agree that someone is being respectful.

It's okay to start with a generalized expectation like mutual respect, but don't stop there. Take it a step further and ask, "What would we see or hear—what would we not see or not hear if we were showing respect for one another?" One of your answers might be, "We wouldn't hear team members interrupting each other." Another might be, "We would see only one person speaking at a time during a team meeting and everyone would be paying attention to that person."

These behaviors, translated into ground rules would read, "Do not interrupt; allow all members to finish their statements before responding," and "One person speaks at a time; no side conversations during team meetings."

A ground rule of one of my teams is "Don't say this will never work." Instead ask, "How can we make this work?" They came up with this ground rule after discussing what positive attitude would look like and sound like. Make your ground rules as behavior-specific as this and they will work for you.

2. *Use the consensus decision-making process to develop your ground rules.* Majority rule is out of the question. This is one of those decisions that requires a high level of commitment from all members. Everyone must agree to support the ground rules actively. As Bruce said, all members must be willing to monitor the team's performance against the ground rules. This means that every member feels comfortable in calling a time-out to let a member know that his or her behavior is contradicting a team ground rule. Consensus is one more factor that makes your ground rules come alive.

3. *Keep your ground rules visible.* Moses had the right idea when he chiseled the Ten Commandments onto a tablet and made them visible to all. Do the same with your ground rules. We seem to pay closer attention to things that we write down and keep in sight. Some teams print their ground rules on poster board to hang in their meeting room. Others make sure every member has a copy of the ground rules and they read them at the beginning of every meeting. Be creative; do whatever it takes to keep your ground rules visible.

4. *Call time-out when a ground rule is broken.* Sports teams have ground rules, above and beyond the rules of their particular game. There is an understanding between the coach and the players that the coach will stop the action by calling a "coach's" time-out when players' behavior is outside the ground rules. Your work team is a little different when it comes to reinforcing the application of your ground rules. Don't leave this responsibility up to your team leader. He or she is the head coach, but for your ground rules to be effective, every member

must play the role of assistant coach. It's best not to assume this. Include a specific ground rule that says, "It is every member's responsibility to call a time-out to remind another member that he is breaking a ground rule.

5. *Revisit your ground rules from time to time to make sure they are still working for you.* You may need to add some to counteract dysfunctional behaviors that have surfaced. You may be able to eliminate some because they have now become good habits.

The Note in Part Three, "Simple but Powerful Team Ground Rules," provides a sample list of ground rules that many of my client teams have established. Ground rules are truly a team's guiding light. But remember: every team must establish its own.

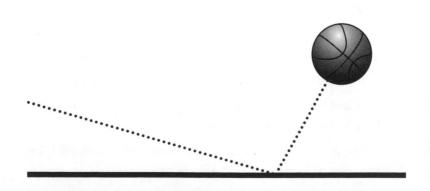

PART 2

Being a Valuable Team Member

If there is one prevailing theme throughout this book, it is "Take responsibility." Although the team leader is held accountable by senior management for establishing and monitoring team performance measurements, *all* team members are responsible for their team's success. If your prior experience was as a member of a work group, your contribution was to get your work done. Your contribution as a team member goes far beyond the work itself. The eight Notes in this Part provide you with advice about how you can interact with the people on your team more productively and offer you tips on how you, as an individual team member, can facilitate constructive team dynamics.

Who Is Responsible?

Years before I started my own business and long before I ever headed up a department, I was a department member. During this period I'm ashamed to report that I became obsessed with inventing ways to get out of attending our ghastly weekly meetings. Those times made me think of the days when I taught physical education, and I began to have a new appreciation for my students' extraordinarily creative minds. They could dream up some of the most creative reasons imaginable for being excused from class. I remember one of the best: "My sneakers were totally covered with a spider web this morning and I was afraid to touch them because the spider might still be in them."

These department meetings were as much a plague to me as gym class was to my students—so much so that I may have even topped my students in inventing outrageous excuses for not being able to attend, even though they didn't always work. I also did my fair share of moaning and groaning, right along with my red-blooded co-worker bees. We'd leave the meeting and in unison say, "What a waste of time."

Our department head was a technological genius and we all admired and appreciated his brilliance. He was also a very kind and caring man. But when it came to leading a meeting, the bright lights went out. He was woefully dull. He would open with, "So how are things going?" We'd all respond, again in unison, "Very well," and hope vainly that he'd say, "Well, all right, the meeting is adjourned." A one-minute, stand-up meeting would have been perfect. It never happened. Next, he would distribute copies of the notes from his staff meeting of the day before and proceed to read them to us. There was a time when I enjoyed being read to; I think I was about four years old.

Then, "Do you have any questions?" Not wanting to prolong the agony, we would again respond in unison, "No." We had our chorus responses down pat. Occasionally he'd shock us and ask for a status report on a particular project. That done, it was time for assignments. He'd tell us what he wanted each of us to do. "Any questions?" A resounding chorus of "No." The meeting which had started one hour earlier was adjourned. Our voices lowered now to a whisper, sang out, "Thank heaven; the meeting is over."

These meetings were so ineffective as to be painful, but none of us ever tried to influence a change because we felt we were not responsible. These were not our meetings. They were his meetings. Some of us learned to cope with them and, thanks to my gym students, I had learned how to get excused from them.

Your team meeting is, or should be, an entirely different ball game. It *is your meeting* and therefore it *is your responsibility* to do whatever is called for to make it effective. Team meetings are not something that happen to you; they are something that you make happen. Your team leader, as a participating member, has a piece of the action but he is not solely responsible. And if your team has established a role called "meeting facilitator," that person might take the lead in reserving the meeting room, distributing the advance agenda, or similar tasks, but he is not totally responsible. *Every single team member is responsible.*

This is a drastic change in role definition for most team members and for team leaders as well. As a team member you can no longer afford to sit back and be an attendee, spectator, or complainer. You must be a full participant/observer, actively contributing to the content of the meeting and at the same time observing team dynamics and intervening when team members are behaving in dysfunctional ways. It's not an easy job but it most definitely is part of your responsibility as a team member.

If you grew up as I did, viewing meetings as an event that someone else plans and leads and that you attend, this will not be an easy adjustment to make. And if your team leader was formerly a manager or is still a manager, and is accustomed to being in charge of the meeting, the adjustment will be even more difficult. The first step in making the transition to this new role of participant/observer requires a major shift in mind-set by all. To behave responsibly, you must feel responsible. And your team leader must also be willing to share the responsibility.

I've known many team members who, at the conclusion of their meeting, sang, *"Deo gratias; ite, meeting est;* wasn't it awful?"* That is, until they realized they could and should make a difference. They started this mind-set shift by talking about it. If you are singing the same song, I suggest you start talking about how your meetings are structured, who decides what the agenda will be, what behaviors are inhibiting the team from accomplishing its intended tasks, and how the team feels at the end of the meeting and why. Then make some decisions collectively about what you can all do to improve it. It could be that you're not singing this song because your team leader has taken full responsibility for your meetings and he's very good at it. I would still suggest you make the transition. Your team leader may not be there for every meeting and as fast as change takes place, you may not have the same team leader tomorrow.

Don't expect to feel comfortable right away with this added responsibility. I remember one team member saying, "It's like becoming a parent for the first time. There's so much to pay attention to. You can't sit back and expect others to make it happen. It's a hard job and it takes an incredible amount of energy."

Check out the following Notes in this Part: "Every Player Contributes to the Process" and "Summarizer, Orienter, Harmonizer, and Other Helpful Roles." The tips in them will help you get beyond your current mind-set to the behaviors you need to fulfill your responsibility.

Every Player Contributes to the Process

Your team meeting has two major focal points that require your attention: content and process. Content is what your team is working on; process is how your team members are working together. If I asked you to tell me how your last meeting went and you said, "We discussed the consolidation project, put together a plan for year-end closing, and decided to set up a meeting with the Quality Team to discuss error rates," you would have reported on the *content* of your meeting. Content sounds like those items you would summarize in your meeting minutes.

If your response was, "Discussion became very heated and members stopped listening to one another; the energy level was very low, and a lot of time was wasted talking about unrelated topics," you would have described your team's *process*. In other words, process is a description of how members behaved during the meeting. Another word used interchangeably with process is *dynamics*.

There may be times during a team meeting when you feel you can't participate because you're not conversant with the topic being discussed. Just because you can't contribute to the content doesn't mean you can't contribute at all. You are in a perfect position to observe and facilitate the team's process—and that's where teams need the most help. Teams generally do fine with content; they usually have the right items on the agenda and enough contributing experts. Ineffective meetings are usually the result of dysfunctional team dynamics or process. The entire team is responsible for the success of your meeting so *all members should play an active role in facilitating healthy dynamics.* But when

47

you are not engrossed in the content of the meeting, you have the advantage of perspective; you can concentrate solely on process.

How do you know whether a team's process is functional or dysfunctional? If the team strikes a balance between satisfying both its task and relationship needs, it has a healthy, functional process going. Members behave in ways that facilitate getting the job done and at the same time make members feel valued, respected, included, and energized. Members leave the meeting saying, "We were very productive and I sure do like being a member of this team." When there is an imbalance between task and relationship need satisfaction, or not enough attention paid to either, the team's process is dysfunctional. If you hear members saying, "We got a lot of things accomplished, but I can't stand the way members treat each other," it's a sure sign that the team hasn't paid enough attention to its relationship needs. And if you hear, "We are so cohesive; just like a family. But we sure didn't get much done," the team has slipped on the task side. And if ever you should hear, "Another waste of two hours—nothing accomplished. Why can't people at least be civil to each other?" you know there is much work to be done on both the task and relationship sides of the equation.

Learning how to observe your team's process and intervene appropriately takes time and practice. If you randomly try to watch everything, you'll see nothing. *The key is to train your eyes and ears so that you can focus your observations.* A good way to start focusing is to *become acquainted with a few specific team facilitation roles,* also known as intervention behaviors. Then look for the appropriate situations during your meeting to apply them. In other words, first learn what the helping behaviors are, and why and how they help. Then you will more easily see places where you can be helpful, as explained in the next Note, "Summarizer, Orienter, Harmonizer, and Other Helpful Roles."

Summarizer, Orienter, Harmonizer, and Other Helpful Roles

Over dinner in the course of a team coaching session about eight years ago, I was determined to create a mnemonic device that would help teams remember the task and relationship facilitation roles that contribute to team effectiveness. The terms themselves have been in widespread use for some time, but no source I consulted had organized them in an easily memorable way. Two glasses of Chardonnay later, I came up with an acronym in the form of a woman's name: SOFI HAGE. I know it's obscure but, hey, I had to use the letters available to me. So now I tell teams, "Don't forget to take SOFI HAGE to your meeting. Put her to work and I guarantee she will make a significant contribution to your team's progress and success."

The exhibit "Team Facilitation Roles" introduces and explains SOFI HAGE. The name comes from the first letter of each of the task and relationship roles.

It's important that all team members understand and employ each of the four task and relationship roles listed in the exhibit. I mention many of them throughout the book as I describe how the techniques they embody can prevent or correct some of the more common team dysfunctions. Let's spend a few minutes examining each of them.

The *Summarizer* urges the group to acknowledge consensus and reach a decision. When team members are wound up like the Energizer Bunny, the Summarizer breaks in with, "It seems like we're all in agreement with the parts of the program that need to be changed; can we

TEAM FACILITATION ROLES

Task	Relationship
Summarizer	Harmonizer
Orienter	Analyzer
Fact Seeker	Gatekeeper
Initiator	Encourager

move off that topic and discuss specific changes to be proposed?" By asking for verbal agreement with the summary, the Summarizer helps the team get past one decision and onto the next decision point. The Note on talk-a-thons in Part Three will help you appreciate the role of the Summarizer.

The *Orienter* prevents the team from wandering too far from the topic at hand; he or she brings them back and focuses them again when they do stray. This redirecting should not be done abruptly as in, "Hey, we're way off here; let's get back on track," or "David, you just took us off topic again," because you don't want to introduce a negative effect into the relationship side of the equation. A useful and neutral way to intervene is with the question, "Are we off topic right now?" The Note in Part Three, "Off Course and Down the Road of Totem Poles," helps you see when this kind of wandering takes place.

The *Fact Seeker* tests reality to make sure the decision the team is about to make is doable. This team member always wants more information and is quick to point out the difference between a fact and an opinion. The Fact Seeker is also very helpful in pointing out when a team does not have all the information it needs to make a good decision. The Fact Seeker will suggest that the team get more data before proceeding. He or she is also good at checking the decision-making boundaries of the team, asking, "Do we have the authority to make this decision?"

The *Initiator* gets the team started on the right foot by always beginning discussions with the question, "How should we approach this task?" Getting agreement on a game plan before starting to work on the task itself is the guaranteed remedy for the "ready, fire, aim" team disorder examined in "Agree on a Game Plan" in Part Four and is the distinguishing characteristic of the Initiator.

As you can see, when you play the Summarizer, Orienter, Fact Seeker, and Initiator roles, you contribute to your team's productivity by moving the task along to completion. Play the following relationship roles to ensure that team members feel valued and respected and you will make a major contribution to your team's cohesiveness.

The *Harmonizer* realizes that conflict is inevitable and that if left unresolved, it is the biggest barrier to a team's achieving health and success. The Harmonizer calls the team's attention to a conflict (especially if team members haven't wanted to acknowledge it), by saying something like, "Let's be honest: we've got some strong conflicting feelings about this issue. What steps can we take to resolve our differences?" The Harmonizer is also able to focus discussion on meeting specific needs as a way of mediating conflict. More help on mediation is given in Part Three: "When You Reach an Impasse, Talk About Needs" and "'Hey, No Problem.'"

The *Analyzer* watches for changes in the vital signs of the team and brings these changes to the attention of the team (discussed further in "Take a Team Pulse" later in this Part). The Analyzer is the team member most likely to ask, "How is everyone feeling about how we're working together?" or "It seems we've lost our energy; what is happening?"

The *Gatekeeper* is concerned primarily with team communication and participation. This member makes sure all team members are actively listening to each other and understanding each other's messages. The Gatekeeper paraphrases messages to make sure that everyone is on the same wavelength and prevents the dreaded Whack-a-mo, discussed in Part Three, by ensuring that every idea is understood by the group before being discredited or discarded. The Gatekeeper invites quieter members to participate and makes sure that more active members don't dominate.

The *Encourager* builds and sustains team energy by showing support for people's efforts, ideas, and achievements. If the Gatekeeper focuses on making sure the content of team members' ideas is clearly understood by all, the Encourager emphasizes members' participation by giving verbal approval: "Good point—that's a great idea." This is another role that prevents Whack-a-mos and in general helps people to feel valued.

It is extremely important that every member be ready and able to intervene as a facilitator. If you were an eight-member team and each person had a delegated responsibility to wear one of the SOFI HAGE hats and intervene appropriately, you would see a significant increase in your effectiveness. But you can do better than that by having each member wear all the hats and thus provide maximum facilitation coverage.

Learning the eight different roles may seem at first like an overwhelming challenge to you and your teammates, but you'll probably be surprised to find that some team members are natural at orienting or encouraging, or that some easily assume the role of summarizers and gatekeepers. To have all eight roles covered may just be a matter of learning a few more facilitation behaviors. I know you can do it and as a team you'll be glad you did.

There is a fun way for the whole team to learn how to function in these facilitation roles. Try it out for ten meetings and before you know it, every member will be able to wear all the SOFI HAGE hats.

1. Post the SOFI HAGE roles on a flip chart in your meeting room so they are visible to all the members.
2. Discuss the roles as a team to make sure that everyone understands each role and knows when to apply it. For example, if the team is off topic, play the Orienter role.
3. Start your meeting with the understanding that whenever any member sees a situation that lends itself to one of the facilitation roles, that member should play the role. In addition, any time a member notices a teammate applying a role, the member should name the role and offer positive reinforcement by calling out "Great orienting." Each time a member plays a role or notices one being played, he is awarded a point.
4. The two members with the highest number of points at the end of the meeting receive a traveling "Great Facilitating" trophy, which they keep until the next meeting.

Recognize Your MVP

When a sports team wins a championship, they follow a time-honored tradition of recognizing their most valuable player. This is the player who, for that game or series of games, gave a stellar performance. It's a nice touch. The team is also generous in lavishing public praise on their MVP during the post-game interview. In my own sports career, no praise pleased me so much as when a fellow teammate would say, "We couldn't have done it without you." We should apply this same practice in our work teams because it is an important investment in team building.

From time to time, you will have a member who puts in extra hours or who applies his or her particular talent to a project to make it a winner. This was the case with a project team I coached recently. The team had just completed the first phase of the project, which had involved a significant amount of research. Their product was a twenty-page report of recommendations to management. Although it had been a true team effort, Janet had put considerable extra effort into the project. Because she had a special talent for writing, she had volunteered to author the report and had done a masterful job. Management was so impressed by the report, which had been signed by all the team members, that they presented the team a special award at their quarterly employee meeting.

During one of our breaks, Janet voiced a concern to me that her commitment to teaming, which had once been very high, was now faltering. When I asked her why she thought that was happening, she responded, "Well, everything is the team, the team, the team. There doesn't seem to be any appreciation for individual effort any more. I mean, here we just received this award from management and that's great. But no one seems to care that it took me two weeks to write that report and that I did it at home, on my own time. I certainly don't expect any formal reward for that, but a simple thanks from my teammates would have been wonderful."

Janet deserved special recognition from her team. When she didn't get it, her motivation and her commitment to the team were severely affected. As she said, it doesn't have to be anything formal; just a "thank you" at a team meeting would go a long way. I remember a team who recognized its MVP by writing him a thank you note, which they published in the company newsletter. I saw another team give its MVP a standing ovation at the end of their team meeting.

In a team-based environment, it's management's responsibility to reward team performance. It's the *team's* responsibility to recognize and acknowledge its stars. Be generous with your praise; it's a powerful motivator and it costs nothing to give.

Get New Players into the Game

When a new member joins your team, the team's rhythm and sense of equilibrium are going to be affected. No matter where you are in your growth cycle—even if you have reached the high-performing stage—you will need time to regroup. Some of the regrouping tasks you'll engage in, like clarifying goals and roles, are reminiscent of the forming stage, so you may feel like you're going backwards. Rest assured that you're not. It's all a part of regaining your stability and the sooner you can assimilate your new members, the quicker you will return to your current levels of productivity and cohesiveness.

I am currently working with five employee involvement teams that rotate members in and out every nine months. Knowing that this rotation is a given in the design of their teaming structure, I suggested that they create a plan for assimilating new members.

The first step of their game plan was to define what they meant by successful assimilation. Staying with the concept of paying equal attention to the task and relationship needs of the team, they decided that when new members became productive (able to contribute to the achievement of team goals) and felt valued and included (reported feeling good about being a team member), they would consider their assimilation activities a success.

The team generated some fine ideas, which they have implemented through two rotations. Based on their definition of success, with which I wholeheartedly agree, they have scored high marks. With their permission, I have reproduced here a number of their assimilation ideas. Try some of them. Your new members will soon feel a strong sense of bonding and identity with your team and will shortly be making real contributions—and your team will be right back in its productive pattern.

- About two weeks before the new member is scheduled to join the team, send her a handwritten, personalized note saying you are looking forward to her coming on board.

- The morning of the first day she officially joins the team, have a helium balloon printed with "Welcome" delivered to her work area.

- Post an announcement on a centralized bulletin board or submit a press release to the employee newsletter about her joining the team.

- Early in her first week's tenure on the team, schedule an off-site, get acquainted, team-bonding breakfast or lunch.

- Design some simple ice-breaking activities for this event, such as talking about hobbies, interests, most embarrassing moments, most victorious moments, favorite foods, baby pictures. Present her with any logo team accessories currently in use, such as a T-shirt or sweatshirt, cap, paperweight, or pen.

- Assign one team member as her buddy. This veteran member is responsible for making sure the new member is introduced to critical team contacts and has access to the training she needs to begin to contribute.

- During the first week, schedule a meeting dedicated to explaining the team's noble purpose and specific goals, team members' roles and responsibilities, and the team's ground rules.

- During the first week, bring her up to date by giving her a folder with minutes from the last six months' meetings and status reports of current projects. Her team buddy is responsible for reviewing this material with her.

- Find out what special skills and knowledge she brings to the team. Include these in a presentation of total team expertise.

- Start her on a project by the end of her first week on board.

Take a Team Pulse

Under the standard operating procedure shared by most doctors' offices, an assistant checks your temperature, pulse, and blood pressure before you ever see the doctor. My only complaint is that unless you ask for those numbers, she doesn't generally share them with you. The information she seems very willing to share is your weight and she shares that with everyone within earshot. Have you ever noticed that the scale is almost always in the hallway between the examination room and the reception room? Even the most soft-spoken assistant yells this number out for all to hear. No wonder my pulse is racing and my blood pressure is off the charts by the time I get into the exam room!

All kidding aside, this standard practice of assessing vital signs makes good sense. The doctor needs this information to conduct a thorough analysis of the patient's condition. There's also an emerging trend in the medical profession for doctors to involve patients actively in the diagnostic process. After taking notes on all your symptoms, they ask, "What do you think is wrong with you?" Their theory is that most patients know their bodies sufficiently well that they can, with a fair degree of accuracy, identify their illness.

What does all of this have to do with teams? For one thing, a team is a living, breathing organism and just like any human has vital signs that warrant monitoring. Energy level, participation, ability to focus, level of productivity, attendance at team meetings, and morale are some that come immediately to mind. All team members need to watch these life signs closely. If you notice a major deterioration, it's important to determine what's causing the change. That brings me to the second connection to the medical profession: most team members have the answers—they know what's wrong with the team. It's just that no one has bothered to ask them and, therefore, they haven't taken time away from their work to articulate the problem and discuss the remedy.

As a team member, you can make a significant contribution to your team's health by taking a team pulse. The best time to do this is during a team meeting when all the members are physically together in one place, away from their work area. The first step is to share your observations about the change in vital signs and ask if anyone else has noticed the same thing. In most cases several team members have, but no one has bothered to say anything. The second step is to ask if anyone knows what might be wrong—what might be causing the change. It would sound like this: "I sense that our energy level over the past few weeks is way off. We seem to be dragging our bodies around and just going through the motions. Has anyone else sensed the same thing?" If they have, your next question is, "What's happening? Does anyone have any idea what might be contributing to this?" You will be amazed how this works. Not only does the team know what's wrong, but they almost always know how to fix it.

To return to the medical analogy, how many times have you experienced this: you postpone going to the doctor until you finally feel so miserable you give in and make an appointment. Then while you're sitting in the waiting room, you begin to feel better. It happens to me all the time, and I think to myself, "What am I doing here?" My theory for this miraculous recovery is that I know someone is going to listen to what's ailing me. The same phenomenon happens for teams.

Words Don't Always Mean What They Mean

One-on-one, verbal communication—two people sending, receiving, and understanding each other's messages—is no easy task. Looking at the communication process, the problem seems insurmountable because at its heart is the ambiguity of the very things we depend on to transmit our messages: words. Even the simplest of words has no absolute meaning. People give words their meaning. Each of us has our own internal dictionary, developed over time and based on our unique experiences and perceptions. Here's what happens: I, the speaker, flip through the pages of my dictionary to select words I think are appropriate to get my message through to you, the listener. You consult your dictionary to interpret my words. If perchance our word definitions match, you understand my message and communication occurs. More times than not, however, our definitions don't match. We go bump in the night and end up miscommunicating.

My interaction with Frank, a team leader, illustrates the communication dilemma. Notice I didn't say "my *communication* with Frank" because, as you will see, I never did understand his message. Frank and I were standing in the training room, about to kick off a Scrimmage Training program for his team. He had mentioned that at the conclusion of the program the following day, we would have a cocktail party for the team. I asked him where the party would take place. He said, "I don't know yet but it won't be here. I'll let everyone know tomorrow morning." The following morning, Frank announced that the party would be held in the Preferred Traveler's Club on the first floor of the hotel. I said, "Frank, I thought you said the party wasn't going to be here." "Oh, I meant not here in the training room." By *here,* I thought Frank meant the hotel. There you have it. The simple word *here* meant one thing to Frank and something else to me.

Add more people to the communication process and the difficulty of understanding multiplies exponentially. I remember a team trying to decide on the agenda for their team meeting. I couldn't believe the confusion; it was like a three-ring circus. As it turned out, the word *agenda* was the culprit. For some, *agenda* meant the total design of the meeting, including topics to be discussed, time frames for each topic, assignment of the facilitator and recorder roles, and the approaches to be used for each topic. Other members understood *agenda* to mean the purpose of the meeting. They simply wanted to answer the question, "What do we want to accomplish during this meeting?" Two members couldn't understand why the team was working on an agenda at all. They thought the agenda was already set because the team had previously decided to have regularly scheduled meetings to learn how to work together more effectively. That was the agenda as far as they were concerned. And one member was out in left field without a glove. The team had been having its share of conflicts and he assumed they were there to resolve their interpersonal problems. He took agenda to mean personal, hidden agendas.

The team went around in circles until I called a time-out. "Let's back up for a minute," I said, "and get some agreement on what we mean by the word *agenda*." Agenda is not a complex word, but in this instance it was interpreted very differently by various members of the same group.

If we could align our personal dictionaries, we'd increase our chances of understanding each other. Actually, it's not that difficult to do. It requires two steps. The first step is to stop assuming that communication is occurring. As the listener, don't assume that the message you understand is the same message the speaker had in mind. In fact, if you're going to assume anything, I'd suggest you err on the other side; assume that no message is understood until understanding is confirmed—which brings me to the second step.

The best way to confirm understanding is to hear an instant audio rephrase, better known as a paraphrase. When I am delivering an important message to a team during a coaching session, one that I want to make sure everyone understands, I ask a few team members to paraphrase. When they tell me, in their own words, what they understand, I know whether my message came through. If they misunderstand my message, I now have the opportunity to clarify it. So that's what you can do as the speaker: ask your listeners to paraphrase.

But as the speaker, you shouldn't have to ask. The listener should take on that responsibility and offer to paraphrase voluntarily. Had I been a responsible listener, I would have asked Frank, "Do you mean the cocktail party won't be here in the hotel?" Had the team members, designing their agenda, been responsible listeners, they would have asked, "When we say we're going to design the meeting agenda, do we mean we're just going to decide on the topics we want to cover?" Word definitions would have matched and the net result would have been understanding.

The key to effective communication is paraphrase, paraphrase, paraphrase. If you're not accustomed to paraphrasing, it may feel uncomfortable; it may even seem a bit silly. Some teams have reported that when they first started to paraphrase, their communication seemed contrived and stilted. That's to be expected. Anything new feels forced, but the more you do it, the more natural it starts to feel.

Many of the teams I coach resist the practice of paraphrasing. They frequently argue that "my teammates will think I'm stupid. Worse than that, they'll assume I think they're stupid or that they're not expressing themselves clearly." As a comeback I ask them to stay up late one night and watch "Night Line" starring Ted Koppel.

Koppel appeared on the cover of *Newsweek* a few years back. The article featured him as the most successful television interviewer in the world. The reporter attributes Koppel's success to his uncanny ability to ask the right follow-up questions. When asked about his secret for doing this, Koppel responded, "I listen, most people don't. Something interesting comes along and—whoosh—it goes right past them" (Alter, Michael, and Lerner, p. 50). Watch Ted Koppel in action. Study his natural, spontaneous communication style and what you'll see him do is paraphrase. He has learned the importance of giving and getting feedback in the communications process, and these skills pay him well.

You Don't Have to Be Best Friends

I've heard folks say, "I'm not crazy about the job itself, it's not the kind of work I like to do, but the people on my team are great." There's no question that the personal relationships we develop on our team make a big difference in how we feel about our work and our workplace, as well as our team. If your team members like each other and you've developed friendships, it's probably a pleasure to go to work in the morning. But, contrary to popular belief, you don't have to be best friends to be an effective team. Best friends do not a best team make; best *teammates* make a best team.

Being a best teammate is all about thoughtful behavior. In a sense, it's about treating a teammate as if he or she were your best friend. It doesn't include socializing outside of work, or sharing personal feelings; what it does include is every kind of behavior you can think of that conveys respect.

Think about the ways you demonstrate respect for your best friend. Do you offer help to your best friend when she needs it? Do you listen to your best friend without prejudging his ideas or opinions? Are you sensitive toward your best friend when he is experiencing personal problems? Do you accept your best friend's idiosyncrasies? Do you arrive on time for engagements with your best friend? Do you share information and expertise with your best friend when you know it will benefit her? Do you share in your best friend's excitement and offer praise when he has achieved something?

If you treat your best friends as I do, I'm sure you've answered "yes" to all of the above questions. And I'm sure you can think of many more ways that you show respect for your best friends. That's what it takes to be a best teammate. Start treating your teammates this way and who knows: you may just become best friends. Stranger things have happened.

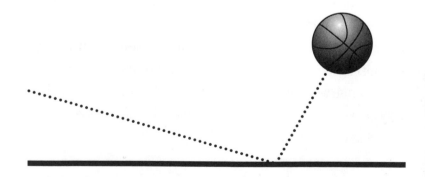

PART 3

Avoiding Common Team Problems

Every team has them—team dysfunctions—and they can drive you crazy. Worse than that, they can sabotage any chance your team has for success because they wear down morale and interfere with getting the job done. You may have a team member who shoots down every idea with a roll of his eyes, or a team that agrees on everything quickly to avoid conflict. The problem may be a team member who seems always to have just one more off-the-agenda story to tell, or a team that lacks one of the most essential components of team success—trust. A winning team must learn how to diagnose their problems and get themselves back on track.

The sixteen Notes in this Part are anecdotes from my personal experiences in turning dysfunctional groups into highly effective teams. I offer them to you as a mirror. If you see your own team in these Notes—good; that's half the challenge. Now, take what they teach you back to your team and practice doing it right.

About Conflict

Teams come up against many obstacles that impede their progress. They may not have the right players, the best mix of complementary skills, adequate support and resources, or effective leadership. These are just some of the hard-core, clear obstacles they face. Highly motivated teams are generally willing to dig in and tackle these barriers; their attitude is, "Here's what's holding us back; let's do something about it." But when teams come up against conflict, team members seem to suffer from paralysis. Uncomfortable with acknowledging the discord, they are powerless to resolve it. This is very unfortunate because conflict is the biggest block teams face; yet it is an obstacle that teams can overcome independently. They are totally empowered to fix it themselves.

There are two types of conflict you will experience throughout the life of your team. They're similar to the conflicts you experience in family life and social life. There's *work-related conflict:* differences of opinion that come about when you're making decisions about things like resource allocation, vacation schedules, role responsibility, work performance, and so on. We could liken these to family squabbles about the budget, child-rearing practices, which in-laws we have Christmas dinner with, and whose job it is to take out the garbage. If you spend time discussing these issues and are truly willing to listen and understand the other person's needs, you can usually come to an amicable agreement (see the Note later in this Part, "When You Reach an Impasse, Talk About Needs"). The second type of conflict is *personality related.* It has to do with behavior. Did you ever think, "If he does that one more time, I think I'll kill him!" I remember a team who felt that way about one of their members whom I nicknamed "Scoop." This man presented himself as the authority on just about any topic by prefacing his opinions with "It's a fact that . . ." In other words, he had the scoop on everything. The team saw red every time this man uttered those words.

A woman on this same team was so facially expressive that she immediately signaled her nonverbal agreement or disagreement with any idea expressed. It didn't bother anyone when she was nodding and smiling her agreement; but when she disagreed, with eyes rolling and lips tightening, the team would come to a complete halt.

These same personality conflicts happen in families and among friends. In those cases, we usually let the offending person know that his or her particular personality quirk really bothers us. A few years back, a friend of mine let me know that my habit of arriving late for social engagements was unacceptable. I appreciated her feedback. Had she not mentioned it, I never would have known how much my tardiness bothered her and it's possible that our friendship would have been significantly damaged. In most cases we don't know how our behavior affects others. Frequently, as was the case with "Scoop," we're not even aware of what we are doing that is so bothersome to others.

The only way to resolve personality conflicts is to let people know what their behavior is and how it affects you. Personality conflicts are more difficult to resolve than work-related conflicts. It's easier to discuss opinions than it is to discuss behavior; but when someone's behavior seriously threatens the team's productivity and cohesiveness, *you must address it.* In my next Note, "The Power of Constructive Negative Feedback," I offer one way to approach this.

The paralyzing effect of conflict seems to be related to the size of the conflict, and conflicts have a way of growing. The longer we try to bury them, the bigger they get. What starts off as a slight difference of opinion becomes "the principle of the thing," and a minor, somewhat annoying personality trait leads to an intense dislike of the person exhibiting the trait. Once the conflict reaches these proportions, resolving it seems almost impossible. The key is to address it immediately. Don't feed conflicts with time. Don't give them a chance to grow.

Conflict is disconcerting; it makes us uncomfortable. Yet if we look at conflict with a clinical eye, we will see it as one of life's natural and neutral experiences. It's only when we attach our view to the experience that it becomes positive or negative. If we view conflict as something that shouldn't be happening on our team, something that will cause our relationships to deteriorate, then it becomes negative. And if we see it as negative, we tend to avoid it, smooth it over, sweep it under the rug, and hope it will go away. Conversely, if we view conflict as something that's bound to happen on any team and see it as an opportunity to strengthen our relationships, then it becomes positive. Seeing it in this light, we surface it, confront it, and take the steps necessary to resolve it. We get what we expect in each case. When we ignore conflict, the net effect is negative. When we resolve conflict, we become stronger as a team.

The Power of Constructive Negative Feedback

At the tender age when we first learned the schoolyard ditty, "Sticks and stones may break my bones, but words can never hurt me," we had obviously not yet heard about feedback. The words people use to describe the effect of our behavior on them can wound us deeply. By the same token, it can be excruciatingly difficult to tell someone he's not carrying his weight or that his behavior is hindering your performance or that it is just grinding your nerves.

This is the stuff that interpersonal conflict, hurt feelings, and team dysfunction are made of. I consider these tips on feedback—both getting and giving—to be potentially the most valuable advice in this book. First, a few definitions.

Feedback is a described reaction to someone else's behavior. Feedback is *negative* when the effect of the behavior is negative; feedback is *positive* when the impact of the behavior is positive. Whether feedback is negative or positive, it should be given in a way that is useful to the recipient—that is, it should be *constructive* feedback.

There are ways to deliver negative feedback without having it come across as an attack, and when you present it in this constructive way, it truly is a gift. Constructive feedback strengthens relationships, enhances communication, and resolves conflict. When we first attempt to use this model for giving feedback, it pays to plan our remarks in advance; left to our own devices, we're likely to blurt out a personal attack. Then we have to backtrack, apologize ("I didn't mean what I said"), and try to get the relationship back on track. That's what we're trying to avoid.

My own learning experiences with feedback have not been without pain. Years ago, I had a golfing buddy who had a very loud voice and a penchant for story-telling. She was very dear, but it seemed that she always had to start one of her stories right in the middle of my back-swing. I found this maddening, and it definitely affected my play. I kept finding reasons not to say anything to her; but finally her behavior bothered me so much that I stopped inviting her to play golf with me and when she invited me, I made an excuse for not joining her.

Why didn't I say something to her sooner? Why did I let this conflict fester? For precisely the same bad reasons you don't say anything to your teammate who is driving you crazy: I was afraid she'd "take it wrong"; she'd think I didn't like her, and matters would just get worse. So I didn't say anything and matters certainly did get worse: we completely lost touch.

In the years since that incident, I've mended fences with my chatty friend and I've practiced my feedback techniques. Here are the five steps I recommend for giving constructive feedback:

1. Let your teammate know you want to give him feedback. This accomplishes two things: first, it focuses the communication so that he can prepare to listen; second, it gives him an opportunity to postpone the discussion if the timing is bad for him. If he does want to postpone, be sure to schedule a specific time. Don't settle for "later."

2. Describe the situation when the behavior occurs. It's important to keep your feedback in precise context. For example, "Sally, when we played golf yesterday there were three times when . . . ," or "John, twice this past week . . ." Stay away from words like "always" and "never." If you say, "John, you're always late for our meetings," John will likely

become defensive and attempt to prove that there have been occasions when he was on time.

3. Describe your teammate's behavior. Behavior is an act we can see or hear; anyone who witnessed it would agree that it happened. Steer clear of colorful modifiers that impute motive or attitude, such as "uncooperative," "surly," or "disrespectful." Just tell the person exactly what you saw or heard her do. For example, "Sally, when we played golf yesterday, there were three times when you began talking in the middle of my backswing." Describing behavior neutrally does not come naturally to us; we are more apt to head for colorful, blaming words like, "Sally, you never think of anyone but yourself," or "Sally, you're so inconsiderate."

Describing the person's behavior keeps the feedback objective and prevents it from becoming a personal attack. Sally can listen to me describe her behavior; but she would quite understandably become defensive with short-cut emotional language.

4. Describe the consequence or impact of the behavior. A consequence can be an observable result or it can be a feeling. This description is especially important because behavior itself is often neither positive or negative. We can behave the same way with two different people and have a positive impact in one case and a negative effect in the other. When I'm in "teacher mode," trying to speak slowly and clearly to introduce a new concept to a group, one member may say, "I'm having trouble grasping this information, and I really appreciate your patience." Another member of the same group may tell me, "Maureen, when you speak so slowly, it makes me feel like you're talking down to us; I resent it, and I just tune out." It's important here to refer to the

behavior and not to the person; use the neutral pronoun: "*it* makes me feel . . . ," and not "Maureen, *you* make me feel . . ."

5. Offer a suggestion or recommendation—for example, "Sally, I'd appreciate your remaining quiet while I'm swinging," and "John, it would really help if you could be punctual at our meetings." There may be times when you don't have a specific suggestion. It's important in these cases to suggest that you get together to discuss and resolve the issue: "I don't know what to suggest here, but between the two of us I'm sure we can resolve this. I'd like to do that now or set a date for us to get together."

If we give negative feedback in this constructive manner, we increase the probability that the person will receive the feedback without becoming defensive. If we have stayed objective, been specific, and confined our objection to the behavior, not the person, we have done our best.

Receiving Feedback

No matter how tactful we are, however, there are no guarantees of success. Sooner or later, we are going to be on the other end of this interaction, so it's equally important to know how to receive feedback. When this time comes, the following rules can help.

1. Make this mental note to yourself: *Do Not Defend!*
2. Paraphrase the message to confirm that you have understood. For example, Sally might say to me, "Maureen, I understand that you take golf pretty seriously and you really need to be focused. My talking

while you're swinging really throws you off and you want me to stop doing it."

3. Thank your teammate for the feedback. When someone gives you feedback in a constructive way, it is meant to be a gift. The person values the relationship enough to want it to be positive and doesn't want your behavior to get in the way. When you consider the anxiety of giving someone negative feedback, you have to appreciate the value of feedback as a gift: "Maureen, thanks for letting me know."

4. Comment on the suggestions/recommendations. Let your teammate know whether changing your behavior is something you are willing and able to do, as in, "Moe, that's no problem to me; I can do that," or from John, "I'm afraid I can't be on time for our Tuesday meetings."

5. Offer facts if appropriate. At times there is an understandable reason for your teammate's behavior; remember that these reasons must be facts, not opinions. John may reply, for example, "For the last three weeks I have had to attend special meetings on project XYZ which, as you know, is important to our team. These meetings have run late and that's why I've been late for our team meetings. There's not much I can do about this but believe me I do consider our team meetings top priority."

It's very important that paraphrasing be the first step in the process and offering facts be the last. That's because we need first to make sure we understand the message; if we offer the facts up front, there's a good chance that our approach will come across as being defensive.

Positive feedback should be given in the same constructive manner. When people do something with a significantly positive impact, you want them to know precisely what they did so they can repeat the behavior. Too often we just say, "Hey, great job," or "That presentation was really super." Although that's music to our teammates' ears, they have no idea *why* their presentation was so effective and haven't learned anything from the feedback.

Whether the feedback is positive or negative, we need always to deliver it constructively and receive it as the gift it truly is meant to be.

When You Reach an Impasse, Talk About Needs

The tone of a work-related conflict can become so emotional and high-pitched as to make resolving the conflict seem impossible. The conflicting parties dig in and hold their positions so tightly that it appears they won't budge unless they get what they want. If you've ever been part of such an entrenched conflict, you know the feeling. The effect is like being in the middle of traffic gridlock: it appears there's nowhere to go.

This was the case with a customer inquiry service team I worked with recently. The team was responsible for responding to telephone inquiries from customers seeking product information. The majority of the members wanted to institute what is known in the industry as a peer "call coaching" program. Two members were adamantly against the program, which called for team members to listen in randomly to each other's calls, without prior notice, and take notes on the transaction as the basis for a peer critique later in the day—an educational eavesdropping of sorts. "We want the program; you don't want it," said the majority. "That's right," said the two holdouts. "That's where we stand. No way will we be part of this program!" Both sides stared at each other in silence; neither was about to budge.

As a team member, whether you're part of the gridlock or you've taken on the role of harmonizer in an attempt to mediate the conflict, the first thing you need to do is take a deep breath, then start probing for needs. When we become emotionally invested in getting what we want, we often lose sight of why we want it—and the reason we want anything is to satisfy a need. One of the secrets to resolving conflict is to find out what people need. It's very possible to satisfy a person's or a group's needs without necessarily giving them what they claim to want. The easiest way to find out what people need is to ask, which is what I did in the case of the "call coaching" conflict. "It seems we've reached an impasse, but let's try to work through this," I said. "What need will be satisfied for you if we go ahead with the call coaching program? In other words, why do you want it so much?"

The proponents responded, "It's a great program. We've talked with others who are using it and they say it's a very quick and effective approach for improving telephone skills and increasing product knowledge. As a team, we need improvement in both areas and we need it fast."

"Okay, we know what you need: speedy development of telephone skills and product knowledge. Let's find out what your teammates need. Why are you so much against the call coaching program? What is it you need?" I asked the opponents.

"We need privacy," one of them responded. The other said, "I agree we need to improve our skills but having someone listen in on my calls, without my knowing it, is an invasion of my privacy."

These needs had been stated before but had been obscured once the conflicting parties took their positions on what they wanted. Once you bring the needs to the surface, originally or for a second or third time, the trick is to keep the discussion focused on satisfying them. I asked the entire team, "Is it possible to satisfy everyone's needs? We're looking for speedy improvement, which you all agree you need, without invading any member's privacy. Is that correct?" The team chewed on that question and after forty minutes, created their own modified "call coaching" program that satisfied both sets of needs. To protect members' privacy, they dropped the piece of the original design which called for listening in on phone transactions. Instead they agreed that each member would randomly record six of his or her own calls each day. The team would then critique these calls at a peer coaching session each afternoon.

A want and a need are not necessarily the same. I'm not promising that you'll be able to resolve every work-related conflict by exploring and satisfying needs versus wants, but very often this approach works.

Team Process Is Confidential

There's an old newspaper axiom that bad news crowds out good. We surely see the proof of that in our media day in and day out; it seems that newspapers, radio, and television can't tell us often enough about what's going wrong. There are nights when I refuse to watch the news. I prefer to go to bed ignorant but without a headache. Wouldn't it be nice if the media would give equal coverage to the good news? Surely there are successful and inspiring people out there who have accomplished newsworthy things.

This same tendency carries over to teams. Why are some team members so hell-bent on spreading gloom and doom? If you have any of these "team criers" on your team, share this tip with them. They probably don't realize the damage they do when they hang out your dirty laundry for the entire organization to see. The dirty laundry I'm referring to are your *process* issues, those problems concerning the dynamics of *how* you work together. Why should anyone outside the team know about the conflicts on your team, or who's not talking to whom, who's not pulling his weight, or who broke down and cried at last week's meeting? Obviously you need to share *content* issues—that is, information and decisions about *what* you are working on, and that means both the good news and the bad news. But your process issues are your team's business and should be considered confidential information. Teams do need some privacy.

You may ask, "What's the big deal?" For starters, when bad news travels throughout the organization it gets exaggerated and overdramatized as it gets ground by the old rumor mill. By the time the news gets back to the team, it sounds much worse than it really is. The big deal is that the team begins to believe the rumor. What started off as a minor issue now appears insurmountable to the team. The major damage, however, is that any trust that may have existed on the team is truly shaken. It's a little like telling someone something in confidence and then discovering that that person told someone else. Teams assume that this confidentiality exists. Unfortunately, unless it's specifically stated, it doesn't.

As a coach, I take this issue of confidentiality very seriously. For me to be effective, it is crucial that the team trust me and that team members trust each other. So before I even begin coaching, I establish a ground rule with the team around confidentiality. My ground rule states that whatever happens during our session stays in the room. If the team thought I might talk about their dynamics to others in the organization, I doubt that they would bring up the real issues, and their interaction would be stilted. Team members would be playing some sort of artificial, make-believe role, not trusting that they could be themselves.

Ask your "team criers" to stop spreading the bad news. The time and place to discuss your team's process issues is with the team. Better still, why not establish a *confidentiality ground rule* for your team. I guarantee it will stand you in good stead.

What Builds or Destroys Trust?

Every time I take a lesson from my golf pro he says, "Maureen, you won't improve until you learn to trust your swing." Any good golfer will tell you that this is easier said than done. It takes years to develop a swing you can trust. And just when you think you can trust it, you can be undone by one day of "Army Golf" when your ball is flying left, right, left, right, and that trust is gone. Now you're back to square one, checking out your mechanics and once again doubting yourself and your capabilities.

Trust among team members is also critical if a team is to grow and develop into a high-performing unit. Trust takes a long time to develop and is always subject to breakdown. In other words, trust is a crucial, high-maintenance quality of successful teams.

I worked with a team recently who called themselves "The Team from Hell." They indicated that they just couldn't seem to work together; they didn't like each other and, worst of all, they didn't trust each other. I queried them about the trust issue by asking them first to define "trust." After about thirty minutes I realized we were going around in circles. We agreed that trust was difficult to define; they were simply coming up with words that still needed to be defined, like honesty, integrity, confidence, and candor.

So I changed my coaching tactic. "Up 'til now," I said, "we've been engaged in an intellectual, somewhat philosophical discussion about trust. Let's get real here and talk about the behaviors that are getting in the way of your trusting one another." Then I asked them to complete this sentence: "I can't trust you when . . ." I also asked them to use words that describe behavior—some action that someone can see or hear.

The statements they developed were such a treasure and so helpful to them in working through their issues that I asked them if I could include their words, verbatim, in my book. With their permission, here they are. I'm sure they will help your team.

- "I can't trust you when you say you will do something and you don't do it. If you commit to doing something, I expect you to come through."

- "I can't trust you when you don't say what's on your mind. If you don't agree with me, let me know. I hate trying to second-guess you."

- "I can't trust you when you hang our dirty laundry out there for the whole organization to see. When we have 'people' issues, bring them up to the team so we can resolve them."

- "I can't trust you when you talk behind my back about a problem you're having with me. If I'm doing something that's bugging you, let *me* know."

- "I can't trust you when you know it's impossible for you to do something I've requested, but you say you can do it. If you can't do something for me, tell me you can't do it and give me the reasons. I'll more than likely understand."

- "I can't trust you when you don't know the answer to my question and you make one up. If you don't know the answer, level with me. I don't expect you to know everything."

- "I can't trust you when you know in advance that you will miss a deadline, but you don't inform me. If you let me know, I can usually readjust, or if there's a problem, I may be able to help."

- "I can't trust you when you won't share your expertise."
- "I can't trust you when you ask for my input concerning a decision you say you are about to make, and it's obvious you've already made the decision."
- "I can't trust you when you have information that you can and should share and you don't share it."
- "I can't trust you when I tell you about a problem and you blow up. Don't kill the messenger."

If you sense that trust among members on your team is a little shaky, try this same "complete the sentence" exercise with them. It's a good way to get the real issues out on the table. Of course, it's only a first step. Certain behaviors erode trust, so it's critical that the team do something to facilitate behavioral change. One way to do this is to encourage those team members who are experiencing a lack of trust in their relationship to give feedback to each other about the behavior that is getting in the way. It's important that the person giving the feedback do it in a constructive manner and the person receiving the feedback take it nondefensively. (Follow the steps outlined earlier in "The Power of Constructive Negative Feedback.")

Another strategy that works well is to establish specific team ground rules that prohibit the behaviors you identified in the "complete the sentence" exercise. Check out the list in "Simple but Powerful Team Ground Rules" in Part Three and you will see some that have helped teams to develop trusting relationships.

Manage Your Differences

I don't know who coined the phrase "opposites attract," but it doesn't ring true for me. My experience as a team member and coach tells me that opposites clash, at least initially. I am also convinced that if we can get past the noise and begin to look at our differences as making us a stronger whole, we are well on our way to building a winning team. Quite often our differences in personality and style complement each other, once we can see them as strengths.

I learned this lesson firsthand when I was leading a team that was responsible for organizing charity golf tournaments. My co-leader, with whom I had to work very closely, was a very sweet, laid-back Southern gentleman named Lamar. We couldn't have been more polar opposites. The first month we worked together was a total disaster. I thought, "This man is going to drive me crazy." I'm happy to report that over time we have adjusted to each other. We have also learned from each other and now are one of the most successful teams I have ever encountered.

Lamar is as slow as I am fast. I'm sure it takes him an hour and a half to watch "60 Minutes." When we have breakfast meetings, I have finished eating and he is still dressing up his biscuits with butter and jelly. Mind you, we have ordered the same thing but he hasn't even begun to eat. This difference in pace carries over to our golf projects. We have learned that I'm better suited for registering contestants and posting final scores—activities that must be completed quickly. Lamar handles the pre-tournament tasks on which he can take all the time in the world; he prepares the score cards, makes the cart signs, and designs the pairings. Over the years I have also learned to slow down just a bit.

I may not take the time to smell the flowers, but at least now I notice they're in bloom! Lamar will never be a speed demon but in an emergency, when time is of the essence, he comes through like a champ.

Our approach to decision making is also very different. I'm an intuitive, gut-feel decider; if it feels good to me, I say "Let's go with it." Lamar, on the other hand, could have played the lead role in "Dragnet." He wants the facts—nothing but the facts—and lots of them before he is ready to make a decision. The combination of my instinctual style and his analytical style has proven to be a real team strength. If the event were left completely to me, we'd have a great turnout for the tourney, everyone would have fun, but it would end up costing us money. With Lamar constantly testing reality, we have fun and we make money for the charity organization. Together he and I make good decisions.

I chose the title, "Manage Your Differences," for this Note because your team members' style differences are a natural resource for your team. Like any other resources available to you—money, equipment, and information—they need to be managed effectively.

Take an inventory of your resources. Do you have both broad overview and detail-oriented thinkers, introverts and extroverts, analytics as well as intuitionists? Are some of your members "charge ahead folks" while others need to mull something over before acting? How about communication styles: do you have highly expressive members as well as those who are more quiet and reserved?

Once you've identified these rich resources, take a close look at *how* you're using them, or even *if* you're using them. I've seen many teams benefit from discussing this topic at a team meeting. Do you tune people out who are different from you or do you honor and respect their differences? Are members willing to adjust their styles? Are your personality differences getting in the way—impeding your team's progress? Or are you using all these resources to advantage, deploying them at the right time and in the appropriate situations?

Name your differences, honor your differences, and manage them.

Words Are Powerful

One of the fascinations of words is that they are so incredibly powerful. While a picture may be worth a thousand words, a single well-chosen phrase can conjure vivid and gripping mental images. Those pictures evoke strong emotional responses, both positive and negative, which influence our behavior.

People in the "influence business"—politicians, advertising gurus, public relations experts, and professional speech writers—are keenly aware of the power of words and use this power to full advantage. They are veritable word wizards and, unlike the rest of us, they almost never just blurt things out. Their comments are phrased very deliberately and always with a goal in mind. Professional wordsmiths know that the right phrase will produce the response they are looking for in their readers and listeners.

As team players, we need to be more aware of how words are hurting or helping our cause. For example, as simple a word as *team* can make a difference. If you want to feel and act like a team, it helps to *call* yourself a team. Think about it. The word *team* conjures up positive images—people bonding together, rallying for victory, we're in this together, we can do it, striving for the common goal, camaraderie and spirit.

Referring to yourself as the *staff, committee,* or *task force* won't necessarily hurt you; it just does nothing to influence teamwork behaviors. To many, the word *staff* describes persons whose work supports the objectives of the organization—period. When I ask people to tell me what comes to mind when they hear the words *task force* or *committee,* they say, "Something you're asked to serve on, something I'd rather not join, a group of people with a job to do." There's just nothing magnetic, energizing, or inviting about these bureaucratic terms. As I said, no real harm done but no help either.

Sometimes, seemingly innocent words can cause real damage. In my travels as a team coach, I have met a number of well-intentioned team leaders who have learned this lesson the hard way. Let me share their experiences because we can benefit from their mistakes.

Bill headed up a project team, responsible for standardizing the information systems across two organizational divisions. The team was composed of representatives from both the systems function and the business division. About four months into the project, Bill asked me to come in and work with his team. He described the project as on the brink of disaster and the team as seriously dysfunctional. Critical deadlines were being missed, communication had broken down, and team members seemed to be waging a war.

As it turned out, the root cause of the problem was three words. Bill had described the general strategy to the team this way. "We have a highly sophisticated, progressive system in place in Division A. I want you to use this system as the model for standardization. If team members want to make changes to this system, the burden of proof will fall on them to convince the rest of the team to approve the change requests."

Who would have thought that the words "burden of proof" could cause such an intensely negative reaction? But they did. Adversarial lines were drawn from the start. When I asked the team to define the issues, one team member said, "Being a member of this team is like being on trial. If you ask the team to consider a change to the system, you have to take the stand and you'd better be strong enough to withstand a grueling cross examination."

Bill was astounded when he heard how members felt. All he had done was use a figure of speech which for him meant "the team should work together to provide a cost/benefit justification for any proposed change." The interesting point here is that everyone on the team knew that their decision-making process was extremely detrimental to their progress. Yet, no team member brought the issue out into the open for discussion. They all thought that the adversarial approach was the way Bill wanted them to work through decisions. Needless to say, he dropped the term *burden of proof* from his description of ground rules.

Mark, a leader of a small accounting team, complained that his team seemed to be avoiding him. He said, "I don't understand what's going on here. I consider myself a pretty approachable guy. I'm easy-going and a very good listener. When the team performs well, I praise their efforts, but no one comes to me to discuss things. I feel totally isolated at team meetings. I'm there but I might as well not be there. It's as though I'm invisible. They'll answer my questions, but other than that no one really talks to me."

My first ten minutes of observing his team meeting confirmed his perceptions. It didn't take much longer to see what was happening. Mark had unknowingly separated himself from his team by using two words. When directing his communication to the team, he addressed them as "you folks."

I asked the team if this had an impact on them and on their relationship with Mark. Their response was a resounding "Yes." They didn't see Mark as part of the team and felt that his only interest in them had to do with getting the work done. Mark was more than receptive to their feedback and started using "we," "our," and "us." The improvement in team spirit was dramatic.

Russ's goal in forming his Pension Benefits Team was to improve customer service. By integrating the Pension Calculations Team and the Pension Inquiry Team, he had hoped to take advantage of what he saw as a natural synergy between the two functions. He was aware that some barriers had existed between the two teams. Because the Inquiry Team had direct contact with the customer, a general perception existed that they saw themselves as performing the more important function. The Calculation Team resented this. After all, they were the ones who researched all the difficult questions and did all the number crunching so that the Inquiry Team had accurate information to give the customer.

Russ thought this wall would disappear once the newly formed team unified around common goals. It didn't happen. The members were having difficulty seeing themselves as a team. One of the reasons was their continued use of past terminology: "the Inquiry side of the house and the Calculation side of the house." These words reinforced a picture of separation and did nothing to promote feelings of integration and togetherness.

I suggested that since they now had a strong set of complementary skills represented on their team, it might be helpful to refer to each other as "our calculation experts and our inquiry experts." They agreed to try it. Once again, I was amazed at the power of words. Using these words helped bring them together and also contributed to the feeling that everyone on the team was equally important.

Words can and do make a difference. I'm not suggesting that we lose our spontaneity; we don't need to become word wizards. But we do need to pay more attention to the words we use. Unfortunately, this is probably easier said than done and most times can happen only after the fact. Think about the message you wanted to send, the picture you wanted to create, the goal you wanted to achieve, and then check it out. Are you getting what you wanted? If not, check to see whether your words and phrases are the culprit. Ask your audience, the team, if your words are somehow blocking the message you are trying to convey. Marketing professionals do it all the time when a particular campaign they have designed doesn't bring in the results they expected. They learn by their mistakes and stay away from those words in their next effort. You can do the same.

Then there is the flip side of the coin. As a member of the team, if you feel that a co-member or leader is using words that are causing problems, you have a responsibility to minimize the damage. If someone says "you folks" when addressing the team and those words make you feel external to the process or to the team, let him know. It's probably not at all what he intended. But he won't know unless you give him some feedback.

Don't Take It Personally

I often hear team members say, "He takes every criticism of his ideas so personally. Why does he always have to internalize it?" I also hear them say, "It's okay to criticize the idea; you just shouldn't criticize the person." But you can't separate a person from his idea.

Each of us is the sum of our parts. We think, act, create, and can destroy using all we have absorbed through our lives. These parts really can't be separated from the whole. Each piece is still us and the whole is held together in a delicate balance of these parts—ready to fracture with ease. Our ideas are born from our experience and it is nearly impossible to separate an idea from the self. Let me share an example.

Early in my career, I was introduced to a famous artist who invited me on a personal tour of his studio. On display were about one hundred framed paintings. Of these, I counted only fifteen that were signed. Naturally I asked him why so few had his signature. I was somewhat stunned when he replied: "The others are not finished." To my eye they certainly looked like complete paintings, so I asked the next obvious question: "When do you feel a painting is finished?"

His response was a real learning moment for me. "When *I'm* satisfied I've done my best work and *I'm* ready to be critiqued, then it's finished and I sign it." He and his paintings were one and the same, and when his painting was critiqued, he was critiqued. It was a personal thing. He was the work, and the work was he.

I remember this artist each time I hear someone on a team preface an idea with "This is just an idea . . ." or "It may sound crazy, but . . ." or "I don't know if this makes sense, but . . ." What is being offered is an unfinished work. Like the artist, this team member feels that when you criticize his idea, you criticize him. Unlike the artist, your teammate does not have the luxury of withholding his signature. He is asking you to treat his idea with care.

We put forth ideas to have them considered, to have others weigh their merit, their value. With the offering of an idea comes the person. Ideas, as personal creations, need to be handled with care. A negative response or criticism is a personal thing. I am the idea, the idea is I. If an idea is tagged "stupid," what else can I do but feel that I am "stupid"?

Ideas are fragile extensions of fragile creators. When we share an idea we share ourselves, our strength and our vulnerability. People and their ideas are one. Certainly I do not imply that we cannot disagree. We are more cohesive, however, and productive as a team when we critique ideas in a caring way. Put yourself on the other side. Ask yourself, "How do I best accept the criticism of others?" It is personal.

In my own case, when a person truly listens to my idea before critiquing it, I sense that he cares about me and my idea. I saw a sign in front of a small church recently that sums up this attitude neatly: "Talking Is Sharing—Listening Is Caring."

To learn how to criticize your teammate's idea while maintaining and enhancing his self-esteem, read the next Note, "The Deadly Whack-A-Mo."

The Deadly Whack-A-Mo

The single most prevalent and destructive team dysfunction is the phenomenon of assassinating ideas. I call this dysfunction the Whack-a-mo because of the way team members respond when their idea gets killed.

Those of you with rural backgrounds may remember the original Whack-a-mo, a baseball-throwing contest included in many small-town carnivals. As a kid, it was my favorite attraction. I know I am giving away my age, but way back then, for a dime you got three throws. The challenge was to take aim and try to hit goofy stuffed figures set up on shelves. If your throw knocked a doll completely off the shelf, you were awarded one of the big prizes. If you hit a doll with a glancing blow, it would disappear off the shelf only to pop up again. You still scored a Whack-a-mo; you just received a smaller prize.

Some team members are natural Whack-a-mo players. It's so much a part of their nature that I'm convinced they're not even aware they are playing the game. Much to the dismay of their team, though, they play the game very well. No, they don't throw baseballs at their teammates; they score Whack-a-mos by prejudging their teammates' ideas with lightning speed, killing these thoughts outright before they can possibly be considered. Like the Whack-a-mo doll, when a team member's idea gets hit, the member either disappears completely, withdrawing all further participation, or pops back up later with the same idea, even when the team has moved on to another topic. As you can see, the response is either fight or flight.

Because of its insidious nature, the Whack-a-mo can be delivered in many different forms, most of them so subtle that team members don't even realize what's happening. And the negative impact extends far beyond lost ideas: when team members Whack-a-mo each other, they not only zap the team's intellectual capacity—their collective brainpower—but they also drain the team's psychic energy and commitment to the teaming process.

Ideas are assassinated by Whack-a-mos in a wide variety of ways. Here's a very obvious one. You know you've been Whack-a-moed when in response to your idea someone says, "That's ridiculous; where did you come up with that dumb idea?" This is a direct hit. Most team members fall completely off the shelf in response to this one.

The subtle Whack-a-mos are much more difficult to detect and potentially even more devastating. They generally fall into three categories, which I call "the silent treatment," "the disconnect," and "the sleight of tongue."

"The silent treatment" is just that—your idea is met with a deafening silence. Team members report a sick, sinking feeling when they are Whack-a-moed this way. One member said, "When it happened to me I actually started to pinch myself to make sure I existed. I couldn't believe that no one even acknowledged I had spoken."

"The disconnect" is another form of non-acknowledgment. This happens when you present your idea and the next person to speak voices his own idea, without ever referencing or acknowledging your idea. Again, the Whack-a-mo victim begins to wonder if he exists.

Have you ever expressed an idea only to have it, like magic, vanish into thin air? This is the "sleight of tongue," the most subtle and passive/aggressive of all Whack-a-mos. The responses to your suggestion sound like this: "I understand, but . . . ," "Sounds good, but . . . ," "I agree, but . . ." Notice the word *but* in each of these responses. Naturally the Whack-a-mo champ follows the *but* with his own idea and with no further mention of your idea. All you know is that your idea is gone.

Whether the Whack-a-mo is obvious or subtle, the damage is the same. When the Whack-a-mo victim falls off the shelf and withdraws, your team loses her ideas and her energy. As if that's not bad enough, a contagious effect kicks in. As other teammates observe this dynamic, they also begin to withdraw. Mentally they're saying, "If that's what happens when you throw an idea out to this team, I'll keep my ideas to myself." How about the victim who keeps popping back up, coming at you again and again with his idea? You've lost his participation as well. He's not with you; he's been concentrating on how to get the team to pay attention to his idea. Your team now has fewer and fewer ideas, inhibiting your creativity, diminishing the quality of your decisions, and ultimately blocking productivity.

Believe it or not, it gets worse: your team's productivity will suffer even further because the team's morale has been significantly damaged. Victims of the Whack-a-mo have lost self-esteem. Since they feel they have no opportunity to add value to the team, they also lose commitment to the teaming process. One team member summed up these feelings when he said, "Hey, this team stuff doesn't work. You don't need me. I'll just go back to doing my own thing."

As destructive as the Whack-a-mo is, it's easy to stop when it does happen. The key is to recognize the behavior. Keep your eyes and ears open; be alert for Whack-a-mo behavior, especially the subtle kind. When it does happen to you or to a teammate, call a time-out and confront the Whack-a-mo giver. I know some folks who say "Ouch, I've just been Whack-a-moed. Do me a favor and at least listen to my idea. Paraphrase me first so that I know you truly heard and understood the idea. Then you can disagree all you want."

Active listening is the key to preventing the Whack-a-mo. When you actively listen to a person's idea and paraphrase it to his satisfaction, you prove that you want to understand what he is offering; by so doing, you give value to the person and show that you are open to being influenced. It's that simple. Do you have to agree with the idea? Of course not. But when you acknowledge the person by rephrasing his thought, you enhance his self-esteem. Another benefit is that when you truly listen to and confirm understanding of another's idea, you may just find that it has merit and that together you can build on it and make it a great idea.

Now that you know what the Whack-a-mo looks like and understand how devastating it can be, make a concerted effort to eliminate it from your team interactions. A sure-fire way to do that is to establish a team ground rule, as so many of my teams have, that says: "No Whack-a-mos." Be open-minded and receptive to all ideas. Paraphrase to confirm understanding before rejecting the idea.

Don't Confuse Interruptions with Enthusiasm

In addition to coaching teams, I occasionally facilitate meetings for some of my client organizations. It's a nice change of pace. Since my clients know me primarily as "the team coach," I always make a point of clarifying the distinction between my coaching role and my role as meeting facilitator. First of all, in my coaching capacity, I only work with real teams or groups who want to become a team, and I am responsible for developing each member's individual teamwork skills and ensuring that the team understands and knows how to apply teaming concepts. My goal is to bring the team to the point that they are able to coach themselves and improve on their own.

My meeting facilitator role is quite different. I focus on the goals of the meeting. My charge is to make sure that those goals are achieved by the meeting attendees. I participate with my client in the up-front planning of the meeting, from selecting agenda topics and problem-solving methods to meeting room setup. During the meeting, I concentrate on keeping the group focused and participating.

I had a unique experience about a year ago. I accepted an assignment to facilitate a senior staff meeting and although I made it clear that I was there to facilitate and not to coach, I ended up wearing my coaching hat. It happened about thirty minutes into the meeting. I discovered I was facilitating a group of meeting attendees who were unfacilitatable. I know that's not in the dictionary, but it's the best way to describe this group. I'm not exaggerating when I tell you that for the first thirty minutes of this meeting, if any member expressed a complete thought, I missed it. You've heard of sentence fragments; how about thought fragments? Some people never finished an entire sentence. Three members didn't even bother to try; they never uttered a word. I kept inviting them to participate, but they insisted they had nothing to contribute. The meeting was out of control. I was getting nowhere and they were accomplishing nothing.

To these folks, interrupting and being interrupted was as natural as breathing. Even when a person wasn't cut off, because he was so accustomed to being interrupted he would stop in mid-sentence. He'd get the noun and the verb out and then come to a screeching halt. Try as I might, I couldn't seem to persuade these people to stop interrupting. "This is the way we always interact," some members said. "We're a high-energy group, especially when we're discussing something we're all excited about. Besides, we've worked together for so long we can read each other's minds. We don't really interrupt; we just finish each other's sentences." They were convinced there was nothing dysfunctional about their behavior. They actually saw it as a good thing; it was a sign of their enthusiasm.

I was at my wit's end. I had coached teams who felt the same way about interrupting but in my coaching role, I was in a position to influence members to change their behavior. And once they stopped interrupting, they understood how dysfunctional they had been. As the facilitator, I didn't feel this was in my purview.

In my own mind, I knew I couldn't help this group achieve their meeting goals. I was also quite sure that left to their own devices they would fail. So I did what many of my colleagues would term the unthinkable; I opted out of the assignment. I told them I would not charge any fee since I was unable to facilitate their meeting. All I would expect was to have my travel expenses reimbursed. My plans were to board the next available flight, go home to Myrtle Beach, and play some golf.

The group looked at me in horror; and I guess I'm just not a quitter because even as I was voicing my frustration, I thought of another option. I told them I was willing to stay and work with them if they were willing to let me coach. I also explained that as their coach I would establish some ground rules that I would insist they follow and that one of those ground rules would definitely be "no interrupting." I asked them to decide among themselves which option they wanted to go with. I walked out of the room, indicating I'd be back in ten minutes to hear their decision.

I had a quick cup of coffee in the hotel restaurant, called the airline to see if I could catch a flight home that afternoon, and then returned to the meeting room. I felt a tension I had never experienced. It was so quiet that had a feather dropped, it would have sounded like the atom bomb. Then one of the three members who had not contributed to this point spoke up. "We want you to stay and coach. The reason some of us in this room never participate is the constant interruptions. It's been bugging us but we've never said anything because we figured we'd only get interrupted anyway." The group broke up laughing.

With my coaching hat perched firmly atop my head, we forged ahead with the meeting. I reminded the group that my ground rule was "no interrupting" and that as their coach I would reinforce the use of the rule by calling time-out whenever anyone broke it. I also suggested that we establish a cueing procedure to ensure that any member who wanted the floor would get it. We decided that when a member had something to say, he would just raise his hand. Every member agreed to watch for that signal and to recognize that person with a simple nod of the head to let him know that he would be next in turn to speak.

Within the first hour I'll bet I called at least twenty time-outs but each time I did, the member stopped his interruption and, interestingly enough, apologized to the person who was speaking. There was no doubt in my mind that they were catching on, but this was such a deep-rooted dysfunctional behavior for the group that it wasn't about to disappear quickly. At one point one member said, "This business of not interrupting is really difficult for me because I'm afraid that by the time the person speaking finishes expressing his thoughts, I will forget what I wanted to say." I suggested that he jot his thoughts down on a piece of paper. This way he wouldn't have to concentrate so much on what he wanted to say and could pay even closer attention to the person speaking. He tried it and it worked for him.

By mid-morning of the second day, the group had made what I considered miraculous progress. Fewer time-outs were called for interrupting and those that were called were initiated by members of the group. It was exciting to watch them coach themselves and to see how proud they were of their changed behavior.

There is a happy ending to this story. The group achieved their meeting goals very successfully and in the process learned that by not interrupting each other and taking the time to listen, they could achieve so much more. The sequel to the story is particularly exciting. Three months later, they invited me back to coach them again; this time they were a team. Because they had learned so much about working together, and were enjoying it more, they decided to become a team formally.

The moral of the story is, "Don't confuse interruptions with enthusiasm. They are *not* the same. For one, interrupting is disrespectful and when we step on people's words, we may actually dampen their enthusiasm."

The Talk-A-Thon

Once, in jest, I asked an octogenarian friend of mine how her sex
life was. "Actually it's great," she said. "We're into oral sex now. We talk
about it a lot."

Some teams do their fair share of talking about it a lot. Like the
Energizer battery, they just keep going, and going, and going. They don't
seem to know how to bring a discussion to closure and make a decision.
It's no wonder they complain about their ineffective meetings. As one
team explained, "We meet, we talk, we leave, and we accomplish nothing. Then the same topic shows up on next week's meeting agenda."
They are suffering from a team dysfunction I call the talk-a-thon.

You can almost always tell when a team is in the grips of a talk-a-
thon. The first clue comes from a most unlikely place. Take a peek
under the table. Some members are engaged in fancy foot work. With
their toes serving as a foundation, they get their knees pumping in such
a quick, rhythmic, energized motion you can feel the floor vibrate. Most
personality assessment inventories list these knee pumpers as "drivers."
They simply want to get on with it; they don't believe in a lot of discussion in the first place. They've heard enough and feel it's time to move
the discussion along, change the topic, or make a decision.

Another clue is visible above the table. Members who don't usually
doodle are drawing pictures they never believed imaginable and they've
become totally engrossed in their newfound artistic talents. These
members are not necessarily drivers; they believe a certain amount of
discussion is worthwhile but they are becoming impatient and have
lost interest.

There are two more clues. The number of members involved in the discussion has dwindled to maybe two or three and they are beginning to repeat themselves. And those members not engaged in knee pumping, doodling, or talking are very silently rolling their eyes or staring into space. They are trying their best to give a covert signal that it's time to move on.

Pay attention to the clues. It's time to stop talking about it and get closure. Actually, you've gone into overtime; you probably could have finished talking about the topic fifteen minutes ago and made a decision.

As a team member, you can help your team avoid the talk-a-thon by taking on a facilitation role called the "Summarizer." Jump right in when you see this dysfunction arise. To do this you must allow for a healthy amount of discussion and listen attentively to the content. The first part of your job is to take what everyone has said and boil it down into a concise, summary statement. The more you can pinpoint the similar or dissimilar views you've heard, the more helpful you will be.

The television commentators who reported on the presidential debates played the summarizer role excellently. "The three candidates covered these four domestic policy issues. They seem to agree on these four points but are vehemently opposed on these two." The details of the discussion are unimportant at this point; just report the highlights and get agreement on the status of the discussion at this time.

The second part of your job is essential. Remember that your goal is to move the discussion forward so that you can gain closure and ultimately a decision. The best way to get it is to ask for it. "Since we agree that this is where we are right now, are we at a point where we can close on this piece of the discussion and move our focus to this piece? Or are we at a place right now where we can make a decision?"

I had the pleasure of working with a group of systems analysts who were trying to decide whether they should form into a team. Each of them was responsible for supporting a specific functional business team and since they had membership on those teams, they weren't sure it made sense to form their own team. They had a serious talk-a-thon going when I introduced them to the summarizer role. Keith, one of the doodlers, took to this role immediately. He began this way: "We started this discussion by saying that if we could identify some common goals we could all rally around, we had the makings of a team. In other words, we could become a team. We've identified five goals so it seems to me we've answered that question. Would you all agree—we've decided we can become a team?"

Everyone agreed. He had brought the team to a decision but not to the final decision. "Let's close on this part of the discussion then and move onto the next question: Do we want to become a team?"

The group was about to get into another talk-a-thon. Once again he came to the rescue. "I think we're close to a decision. Seems we're saying that emotionally we want to become a team. We want to work on some things together because we'll be able to learn from each other and grow professionally. But we are all concerned about how our client teams will feel. We've worked very hard to gain their trust and confidence; they finally see us as integral members of their team. Are they going to think we're abandoning them if we form our own team? Is that a fairly accurate summary?"

Again the team agreed. "What do you say we move on then. We agree we can be a team and we want to be a team. Now let's tackle the issue of our client teams. Are there some things we can do to maintain their confidence in us?"

Thirty minutes from the time Keith started to play the summarizer role, the group came to closure and made a decision. By the way, they did decide to become a team and the team truly appreciated his contribution. Do the same for your team. You'll be amazed at how many more decisions you will make. Your team will love you for it.

Off Course and Down the Road of Totem Poles

Team members are easily distracted and consequently lose focus during meetings. You've probably seen it happen: one of your team members raises a question unrelated to the agenda item at hand, and before anyone notices, you've wasted precious time discussing something that adds no value. I've named this dysfunction "Totem Poles." It's a phrase my Dad used whenever he was about to take a discussion off track. With his Irish flair for colorful story-telling, believe me, he could do it in the blink of an eye.

No matter what my brothers and I were discussing, he could cut in and render us defenseless with this charming entree, "Hey kids, speaking of totem poles, did I ever tell you about the time. . . ?" Thirty minutes later, totally engrossed in his tales of the Big War or his adventures with Uncle Mike, we would have completely forgotten what we had been discussing earlier. It was fun. He was fun. We always welcomed his diversions.

But when a team member takes your discussion off course and down the road of totem poles, even though it may be fun and even interesting, it is a costly time waster. Just think about it; the time you spend attending your team meeting is time taken away from other tasks you need to accomplish. Multiply this time by the number of members sitting around the table, and it's easy to see that as a team you've lost an immense amount of productivity.

An occasional diversion is fine, but if it happens frequently you have a responsibility as a team member to refocus the team. Play the

Orienter role by asking, "Is what we're discussing right now connected to what we're trying to achieve?" The discussion may not be that far off; you may have just gotten ahead of yourselves. For example, the task at hand might be to identify the *causes* of a particular problem but the team has jumped ahead to *solutions*. Sometimes, however, the discussion strays way off base, not even remotely connected to the task.

Watch for totem poles, play the Orienter role, and keep your team focused. You'll be amazed how your productivity will increase.

"Hey, No Problem"

A team without conflicts is faking it. Like taxes and death, conflict among team members is inevitable. If your team doesn't appear to be experiencing conflict, but your effectiveness is below par, you may be suffering from a team disorder I call "Hey, No Problem." This disorder, left unchecked will be the biggest stumbling block to your team's progress.

The next time you hear a teammate say, "Hey, no problem," check it out. Make sure there really is no problem. This response is often an attempt to avoid conflict. The person responding knows there is a problem but in an effort to maintain some semblance of harmony, she decides to skirt the issue and end the discussion. Your interaction then begins to resemble a duck swimming across a pond. On the surface, you're gliding along smoothly but underneath you're paddling furiously just to stay afloat. It is, of course, a false sense of harmony.

I was called in by a new team leader who said, "I don't know what's going on here but there is an underlying tension and I get the distinct feeling that nobody trusts anyone else. Seems like we're experiencing an inordinate amount of turf protection."

I sensed the tension very early in our "scrimmage" session, called time-out, and asked the team, "What's happening here?" I used my duck analogy to describe my observations of their interaction.

I had unplugged the dam. All hell broke loose as these senior management team members started to dump conflicts out onto the table. They had been saying "Hey, no problem" to each other for five years and had in a sense gone underground to work their own personal hidden agendas. They weren't the only ones working at cross purposes; the teams they led had also taken up the fight. The end result was an extremely dysfunctional organization.

High-performing teams experience many conflicts. They also understand the value of working conflicts through to resolution. Striving to achieve true harmony, they address both personality and work-related conflict immediately. As one member of such a team said recently, "We fight like cats and dogs but it's always a fair fight. It may not look pretty and it can be painful. But because the air is cleared, we're more relaxed, and our relationships are strengthened. In the end, we all win because the team wins. I guess it's true when they say, 'no pain, no gain.'"

This product development project team had learned the hard way, as all teams do during their storming stage. They had had their share of unresolved conflict and had experienced the resulting damage. It was exciting to see how far they had come.

They were discussing their plans for an upcoming presentation to management when two members, who were usually quite vocal, appeared to withdraw. Noticing this, Kevin, a natural Harmonizer, addressed them saying, "Brad and Gloria, you're both pretty quiet today; is there an issue we should know about?"

Brad responded, "It's no problem, but since we've all contributed to this project, I don't understand why only two members are delivering the presentation. No big deal, really." Kevin wouldn't let it go. "No, that's not true; it is a problem and we need to resolve it before we move on." In this case the resolution was an easy one; it was only a matter of reshuffling a few schedules so that all five members could participate in the presentation.

When you sense that team members are attempting to ignore or smooth over a conflict, don't let them take the easy way out. The long-term effect of saying "Hey, no problem" is devastating. As a team member, you can make a significant contribution by playing the Harmonizer. Your primary intervention in this role is to get the issue out on the table and move the team from a problem-avoidance mode to a problem-solving mode. You don't necessarily have to know the solution; use the team resources for that. The Harmonizer helps the team to embrace and welcome conflict as an opportunity to grow and develop. Simply expose the conflict by saying, "We've got a problem here. Let's see if we can work it through." You'll be a healthier team for it.

How the Great Elaborators Finally Got to the Point

I nicknamed a team I was coaching "The Great Elaborators." Each member took a minimum of ten minutes to express himself, even though he had clearly articulated his message in the first two minutes. Observing these people brought back a memory of when my five-year-old daughter had asked me where thunder came from. Sensing that my explanation of God rearranging furniture might be scientifically inadequate, I suggested that she ask her Dad. Rolling her eyes in obvious exasperation, she responded, "Mom, I don't want to know *that* much about it." Out of the mouths of babes! Had she been one of the Great Elaborators, she would have been an invaluable asset.

Their communication style resulted in a Catch-22 for this team. Each time a member began to elaborate, the rest of the team would psychologically tune out, physically stop listening, and consequently lose the original, clear message. Of course we had a fair amount of eye rolling as well. Naturally, the elaborator, feeling that no one was listening or understanding him, would elaborate even further in the hope that someone would grasp his meaning.

This combination of elaborating and tuning out had become a costly and vicious cycle. Lack of listening led to so much misunderstanding that it took the team forever to make decisions. There were even times when some seemingly simple decisions weren't made at all. In addition, some team members had stopped contributing their ideas; feeling that no one was listening, they withdrew. Needless to say, team meetings were unproductive and had become a dreaded event.

Once they realized what was happening, this very bright, creative team came up with a viable solution. They called it their "P" flag. Here's how it works:

Give each team member a small index card with the letter "P" printed on it. This is your "P" flag. When you feel that a member of your team is elaborating unnecessarily and you think you understand his message, raise your "P" flag. This is a signal for the speaker to stop speaking.

It is now your responsibility as the "P" flag raiser to *paraphrase* the speaker's message. Simply play back his message in your own words. If the speaker feels you understand his message, effective communication has occurred and the team moves on. If the speaker feels you didn't quite get his message, he provides the necessary details to clear up the misunderstanding.

If he starts to elaborate again, raise your "P" flag. Continue this process until you have understanding.

Believe me, the "P" flag is an effective intervention; it works. It's a polite, respectful way to say, "I don't want to know that much about it." After observing the Great Elaborators use their "P" flags, I gave them a new nickname: "The Great Communicators."

Team Burnout

You've likely heard marathon runners talk about "hitting the wall." They can predict with a fair amount of accuracy that it will happen after they run twenty miles. They have a little more than six miles to go but for the moment can't seem to muster the psychological or physical energy to take another step. They train with this in mind, preparing in advance to push through the wall.

If your team is in the high-performing stage, you may experience a similar burnout phenomenon, when your energy and spirit are depleted. You are not stuck; you are burned out! Unlike the marathon runner, your high-performing team can't forecast when burnout will happen, so preparation is out of the question. Instead, your team needs to do a little doctoring, some self-administered first aid. The purpose of this discussion is to help your team recognize the symptoms of burnout, determine what's causing it, and prescribe a treatment plan that will work.

Let's take a look at some of the symptoms of burnout. They sound a bit like that old commercial for curing "iron-poor blood." Has your team's energy level dropped to an all-time low? Do your usually enthusiastic teammates now seem robotic, bored, and restless? Does your work day—which once seemed to fly by—now drag on interminably? Is the team spirit you felt in the past now just a fond memory? Do you hear your teammates saying, "I'm totally stressed out"?

What might cause an enthusiastic, spirited, high-performing team suddenly to become mired in such malaise? Over the years, I've seen two primary factors contribute to team burnout: increased workload and insufficient recognition for excellent performance. The team often feels immobilized at this point and because these conditions have been imposed on them, they might feel powerless to change the situation. In actuality, you are not powerless. Now is the time to take charge of your team's psychological health, and there are specific things you can do to remedy the problem. Here are some prescribed treatment plans that work.

When your team gets hit with significantly more work but is not blessed with additional resources, it's time to review work design and distribution. Given your increased responsibilities, it is likely that the way you originally organized yourselves is no longer effective. Take a serious look at who is doing what. Are some team members working overtime while others seem to make it through the day with relative ease? Is there some less critical work that could be assigned to a temporary employee? Also, examine how you approach the work. If you changed the way you do the work, could you save time and increase efficiency? Check out the work itself: are there some tasks you've been doing that may be irrelevant? Are those reports you've been distributing for years critically important—or even useful—to anyone? Does anyone actually read them? If you're not sure, ask. You'd be surprised at how much work can be eliminated. Get out your prescription pad and write, "Work smarter, not harder."

Teams, like individuals, expect and need to be recognized for exceptional performance. If your team isn't getting the recognition from management that you feel you deserve, two things may be happening. First, management may not be aware of your achievements. If this is the case, you need to become your own press agent—start a publicity campaign, hang a banner in your workstation saying, "We did it" every time you reach one of your goals.

Second, it's quite possible that management knows you're doing a great job but it's not a cultural norm in your organization to give praise—an all-too-common scenario. These buttoned-up cultural pockets still exist, especially in large organizations. Whether or not this is true in your workplace, let me share my strong feelings about recognition. If you depend on others for recognition—be it management, your customers, or your colleagues—you will almost always be disappointed. Even when you get a pat on the back, it's never quite enough. So what's a team to do? Provide your own recognition: celebrate your victories, pat *yourselves* on the back.

Before you can celebrate your success, though, you have to realize you've been successful. Be clear about your goals, and then be generous with praise for all who helped achieve them. High-performing teams achieve success because they keep raising the bar. Every time you succeed in clearing the bar you've set, be sure to congratulate yourselves.

Simple but Powerful Team Ground Rules

Over the years, teams I have coached have developed some wonderfully useful ground rules. Here are some of the best and most practical. They are based on common sense and are very simple. It is only when you see them applied that you realize the positive impact they have on team effectiveness.

- Do not have any side conversations during meetings.
- Have fun!
- Be open-minded and receptive to all ideas; paraphrase the idea to confirm understanding before rejecting the idea.
- Forbid Whack-a-mos! (See "The Deadly Whack-A-Mo," Part Three.)
- Begin and end meetings on time.
- Arrive on time for meetings.
- Respond out loud.
- Do not finger-point or assign blame for problems; every problem is a team problem.
- Take turns speaking; only one person speaks at a time.
- Do not interrupt.
- Do not have talk-a-thons; obtain closure on discussion topics and make decisions.
- Make team meetings a priority. Unless there is an emergency, all members are expected to attend.

- Be a team and company ambassador—no bad-mouthing the team, suppliers, or the company.

- Take responsibility for calling a time-out; every team member should do so when he or she notices dysfunctional behavior.

- Ask for help when you need it; doing so is not a sign of weakness.

- Be honest, say what's on your mind—it's all right to push back and disagree.

- Stay focused on the task at hand.

- Celebrate successes.

- Honor commitments; if you say you'll do something, do it. If you can't do something, don't say you can. If you have committed to do something and a problem arises that will prevent you from coming through, let us know in advance.

- If your work is completed and another team member is overloaded, offer your help.

- Don't say, "We can't do it"; ask instead, "How can we do this?"

- If you have a conflict with another team member, resolve it without delay, and without discussing it with others.

- Encourage full participation by inviting quieter members into the discussion.

- Whenever we make a decision, immediately determine the action items necessary to implement. Everyone participates and takes ownership for action items.

- Share failures; it's an opportunity for the team to self-correct and improve.

- Maintain confidentiality—the team's dysfunctional processes are the team's business; don't discuss them outside the team.

- Use consensus for all major team decisions.

- Give positive feedback regularly; tell members they've done a great job.

- Give negative feedback constructively.

- Receive negative feedback non-defensively.

- Summarize and clarify all team decisions at the end of the meeting to ensure understanding.

- Distribute advance agendas stating the purpose of every meeting so members can come prepared.

- Support team members during times of emotional stress.

- Share all the information you have; it's better to err by sharing too much information than too little.

- Stay focused on your team goals and noble purpose by asking, "Are we working on the right things?"

- Always ask these two questions: "How will others in the organization be affected by our decision?" "Who should be included in our planning?"

- Always consider all ideas.

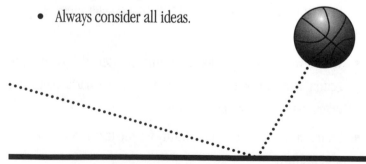

PART 4

Running an Effective Team Meeting

Now that your team is functioning well, what meeting procedures and processes do you need to operate efficiently? Many team members have never had to conduct a meeting; their experience has been limited to listening to superiors present reports or presenting a report themselves. The tips in this Part will help all team members conduct efficient and effective team meetings. The seven Notes provide how-to advice on topics ranging from constructing meeting minutes to using flip charts and staying focused on the topic.

Spend Time Together

You've no doubt heard the expression, "Families who pray together stay together." You have probably not heard this one, since I made it up: "Families who play golf together fight!" But here's one I want you to remember: "Teams who spend time together win." It concerns me when teams report they meet occasionally or even once a month. The more quality time you can spend together, the better.

I encourage all teams to spend at least one hour together at regularly scheduled weekly meetings—not to present or listen to status reports, which tends to be one-way communication, but for discussion. Save your updates for quick fifteen-minute huddles. Since your team meeting is generally the only time all members assemble in one place, make it quality time. Establish an agenda in advance and achieve something together. Use this time to plan, solve problems, design programs, share best practices, or discuss lessons learned from successes and failures. In other words, interact; engage each other in two-way communication. Even if your members are scattered geographically, you can still interact via audio or video teleconferencing.

Frequent interactive meetings are particularly important for start-up teams because members need to begin to bond and get a feel for working together. Many teams also make a point of spending time together outside the workplace. One of the most successful teams I know plans a quarterly "Let's Have Fun" get-together—a picnic, a bowling tournament, dinner out with the spouses, or another such activity. There's a real bonus effect from having fun together and getting to know your teammates as people.

If it's impossible to meet for an hour every week, explore some other option. Maybe meeting every two weeks will work or perhaps once a month is the best you can do. Whatever you come up with, schedule it on a regular basis. If you leave your meetings to chance, they probably won't happen.

Agree on a Game Plan

Rightsizing has become a buzzword for our time. Reductions in force and working "lean and mean" have become standard operating procedures in most work environments. Whatever catch phrase is used, it all adds up to much more work to do with fewer dedicated resources. The name of the game is "Just Do It." And because the competition is so keen, we not only have to get the work done, we have to do it faster than ever before, with better quality, and at reduced cost.

Sometimes teams adopt a "ready, fire, aim" approach as a way of adjusting to this culture. Here's how I've seen it play out. I was coaching a team about to tackle three problems on its meeting agenda. A member started the meeting by saying, "We have a definite problem with our XYZ vendor on delivery." Another member responded, "Well, I have some solutions. Does anyone else have any ideas?" Without waiting for a response, he jumped up to the flip chart and started listing his solutions. The rest of the team followed his lead, offering their suggested solutions. Once the list was completed, they started to discuss what the next step should be. It was a typical ready, fire, aim mind-set: we have a problem, we need solutions, let's get some. They had given no thought to how they might approach the task.

I called a time-out and posed this question: "If I suggested that we all go to Boston tonight and go dancing at some of the swing band hotels, would we just walk out of here and head for Boston without any further discussion?"

"Of course not," they responded. "We'd have to come up with some sort of plan. We'd have to agree on what time to leave, how we're going

125

to get there, which hotels we want to go to, what time and where we will meet. If we didn't plan the trip, we might never see each other in Boston."

"The approach you're suggesting we use for our Boston trip makes a lot of sense to me. It's a ready, aim, fire approach. The first thing we would do is put together a game plan—in other words we would take aim before we fired. The approach you've been using to solve your vendor problem is backwards. You're firing before you take aim."

A six-word question will help you to avoid the "ready, fire, aim" syndrome. Before you begin any team task ask, "How should we approach this task?" You don't have to have a game plan in mind; just ask the team and they will usually come up with something that will work. The member who moves the team toward getting agreement on a game plan before beginning to work on a task is playing the Initiator role. This role is really as simple as asking the six-word question about how to approach the task; yet it is a powerful intervention.

The team with the vendor problem needed the services of an Initiator. Even though the team had completed its solution list, I asked them to back up and start over by having someone play the Initiator role. After ten minutes of discussion, they agreed on the following four-step game plan:

1. Define the problem in specific terms by answering the following questions: What parts is the vendor consistently late in delivering? What is the cost when this happens? Is the vendor always late or are some deliveries on time?
2. Identify the probable causes of the problem.
3. Identify and get agreement on specific solutions to address the causes of the problem.

4. Determine the action items necessary to implement the proposed solutions.

The team had taken dead aim and was now ready to fire. They worked their plan and were amazed to see that the four solutions they agreed on did not appear on their original list. Defining the problem more specifically had really helped. They also expressed a sense of increased confidence as they worked through the steps they had planned. They felt they were going to get where they needed to be.

Lesson learned: no matter how small the task seems or how fast you feel you must get it done, formulate a game plan first (take aim), and then work the plan (fire). Not only will you arrive at better decisions and solutions, but you will also feel more confident in the process.

Everyone Must Respond
Out Loud

Most of us grew up hearing that "children should be seen and not heard." Having parented three children, I have to admit there were times I found it to be an effective ground rule. But silence is definitely counterproductive for teams—so much so that one of my ground rules during a coaching session is, "Everyone must respond out loud." This ground rule serves two purposes: it energizes the team, and it confirms agreement or disagreement, which, in the end, helps to clarify decisions.

You may wonder how verbal responses can create energy unless, like me, you've witnessed silence as the killer. Here's my experience. I've just entered the training room and sitting around the table is a team of six people. I shake hands, introduce myself to each individual, learn everyone's name, and start the session by describing "Scrimmage Training." I want the team to understand that our two days together will be different from other training programs they have attended. I follow up with "Does anyone have any questions?" A few seconds go by—no verbal response. I look around the table and catch two members shaking their head from side to side, which I figure is a "no." I wait a few more seconds but still no verbal response. Ten minutes ago, I entered this room feeling enthusiastic and excited about working with a new team. But at this very moment I feel like someone has injected me with a sedative. I'm wondering if I am alive. I'm also beginning to question whether any of the team members are alive. It's an awful feeling.

Earlier in my coaching career, when this happened I would take a deep breath and forge ahead, psychologically giving myself an overdose of energy. I figured I needed enough energy for me and the team. A few years passed before I realized that energizing the team was not my responsibility. My job was to show them how to energize each other. That was the origin of my ground rule requiring verbal response.

Most teams see the value of this rule immediately. Although members often have to force themselves to respond, they feel the team's energy level rise when everyone begins contributing vocally. Occasionally, though, I do run across some objections: "Well, I'm an introvert. I don't have a lot to say. That's just who I am."

As "coach," I seldom have to respond to such comments because other team members do it for me. Their prodding typically runs like this:

"But you don't have to say much."

"We're not asking for a major personality change. You don't need to be an extrovert to respond to a question verbally."

"What does it take to say no, yes, I don't know, I need more time to think about that, or I didn't understand the question?"

"You owe it to us, your teammates, to say something. We need your energy, and the nonverbal signals just don't do it."

You'd be amazed at how the introverts come alive when they begin to respond verbally.

Besides depleting the team's energy, the other problem with silence is that most teams assume it means agreement—and that's a huge mistake. This misinterpretation can lead to the following scenario: you leave a meeting thinking that consensus has been reached on a particular decision. You go off and start to implement the decision only to meet with strong resistance from a few of your teammates. When you ask what the problem is, they say, "There's been a misunderstanding. We never decided to do that. I never would have agreed to that." That's what can and does happen when we assume that silence means agreement.

We can't possibly know what silence means. It could mean agreement but quite often it means disagreement. It might be an indication that there is a lack of understanding or maybe it's just a lack of interest. God only knows what silence means and she's not telling. The only way we can know for sure what someone is thinking is for him or her to verbalize it.

"Everyone must respond out loud" is a very simple ground rule; but like most simple things, it is very powerful. I encourage you to include it on your list of team ground rules. Feedback from those teams who have done so is very positive. Their meetings have come alive, they are energized, and their decisions are clearly understood by all members, a situation that facilitates a smooth implementation.

Call Your Own Time-Outs

One of my oft repeated messages to members of all teams I work with is, "Every one of you must serve as assistant coach to your team. You must call your own time-outs." I first mention this at the beginning of my second day of coaching. "I'm leaving tomorrow," I say. "I'm not going to be here to call time-out and coach you. Your leader is the head coach of your team but it's your responsibility to assist him in that role. I want you to start doing that today by calling a time-out any time you feel something happening that impedes the team's progress. The impediment could be a conflict that's not being brought out in the open, or a Whack-a-mo one member is using to kill another member's idea, or a talk-a-thon no one is controlling, or maybe a ground rule someone is breaking." Once team members realize they have permission to play this role, they are always amazed at how proficient they are.

I encourage you to do the same. It's critical that you intervene when you see your team or teammates acting in dysfunctional ways. I know this is a lot easier said than done. It's probably even a little scary.

I suggested this to a member of a team I had not coached and he said, "I'm reluctant to do that. I'm afraid my teammates will think 'Who the dickens does he think he is? He's not the team leader. What does he know?' There have been many times when I thought I should intervene but held back because I didn't want my team to think I was Joe Coach."

There are ways to solve that problem. One way is to get every member a cap, with "Assistant Coach" printed in big, bold letters. That's not an inexpensive solution, although it's a good idea. But all you really need is agreement from the entire team to make this assistant coaching role a requirement of effective team membership. If everyone agrees that it's not only okay to call a time-out but that it is mandatory, all members will begin to feel comfortable doing it. Everyone will have permission.

Understand this about calling a time-out: the purpose is to self-correct, to turn dysfunctional behavior around so the team will be effective. Its purpose is not to get the floor during discussion. You use the two-handed time-out signal to help facilitate the meeting. *Don't abuse it,* but please do use it.

All Ideas Aren't Good Ideas But . . .

Our human tendency is to look at an idea in totality and judge it either bad or good. When we assign the "bad" label to an idea, we shoot it down quickly. The end result is lost opportunity; one more idea down the drain.

Like any coach worth her salt, whenever I see team members playing out this human tendency, I have them run a few extra laps. Of course, these are mental laps; I want them to stretch their cerebral muscles. One such incident stands out vividly.

This particular team had been assigned additional workload, which was throwing them into a dither. Their agenda item was to figure out how they could take on the additional work without going into an expensive overtime mode. The team had already rejected three proposed ideas when Martha piped up with, "Look, we spend an inordinate amount of time proofreading and correcting applications. Why don't we tell our clients that we can no longer do that for them. Let them take on some responsibility."

Another member responded, "Martha, are you crazy? This is one of the services they pay for. We have to do it."

I blew my coach's whistle and said, "Okay, you've just killed four ideas in a row. Here's an exercise I want you to do. Let's stay with Martha's idea and see if we can build on it and create a whole new idea."

One member responded, "But Coach, you can't create a good idea out of a bad idea and this idea is definitely bad."

"Humor me awhile," I said; "let's follow four steps for building on ideas and see what happens."

I'll leave the meeting room door ajar so you can peek in and listen to these team members in action. They learned how to look at ideas differently and I'm sure you will too.

1. *Paraphrase the idea to confirm that you understand it.*

One of the members asked, "Martha, are you suggesting that we discontinue reviewing the applications for accuracy and tell the customers that from now on we will input whatever data they send us?"

"No, that's not what I meant," said Martha. "There's no question we have to check the application. I don't have a problem with that. The part of the process that takes so much time is calling the client to get the right information. I'm suggesting that the client be responsible for making the corrections. Let's just mail the application back to him and have him make the corrections."

The member who had paraphrased said, "Oh, I guess I didn't totally understand you."

An idea is often rejected simply because it is not understood. That's why it is so important to paraphrase. But even if the idea is clearly understood, it's important to complete the next three steps.

2. *Look for pieces of the idea that have merit; start with, "What I like about your idea is . . ."*

One member said, "What I like about your idea, Martha, is the notion of placing responsibility on the client. After all, we are providing our customer an important service but he should take an active part in the process. I get the feeling sometimes that our client doesn't realize how important it is that he give us complete and accurate data."

Another member piggy-backed on that member's response and said, "You know, you're right. The client doesn't care about the impact on us, nor should he. But I'll bet if he realized the impact on him when he gives incorrect information, he'd pay more attention to filling out the application correctly in the first place."

One more member said, "What I like about your idea, Martha, is the fact that you've brought up an actual time-consuming activity and those are the types of things we need to look at."

Again, we tend to look at ideas in totality. If we can train ourselves to look at an idea as a set of components rather than as a monolithic whole, we have the opportunity to create.

3. *Identify the piece(s) of the idea that you don't like. Start with, "What really concerns me about your idea . . ."*

One member said, "My major concern about your idea, Martha, is telling our customers that we are going to take something away. Their expectations are well established. We've always contacted them immediately by phone when we detect inaccurate data. I'm putting myself in their shoes and I'd be outraged if you told me the game has changed."

Other members chimed in with the same concern—but interestingly enough, that was the only objection to the idea.

Frequently an idea is rejected based on one major objection. If that concern can be eliminated, the idea may be a great one.

4. *Use the pieces of the idea that have merit; eliminate the major concerns you identified, and create a new idea.*

One member said, "Since our major concern is the client's reaction to having a service taken away, why don't we position it differently. Let's not talk about what we're taking away; let's tell him what we're going to give him—and there's no doubt that the answer is better service. Right now he's getting lots of attention, but it sure isn't good service."

Another member said, "Here's another thought; if we educated the client about the importance of his supplying us accurate data, he'd probably understand the benefits he'd experience by doing it right the first time."

Other team members jumped in: "Maybe, just maybe we could pinpoint the common errors that our clients are currently making and develop an educational brochure or a training video to address those errors."

Their final idea was to create both a video and a handbook that instructed the client, line by line, in completing the application. These products not only explained how to complete the forms, but also stressed why completing it accurately was so important. The team's goal was to reduce the amount of time they spent proofing and correcting applications by 75 percent. When I checked with them a year later, they had achieved a 90 percent reduction in time spent on this activity.

And just think: the team was about to throw Martha's idea down the drain!

Every idea may not sound like a good idea but it's always a good idea to explore every idea. As a team, once you reject a thought, you are at a distinct disadvantage because you can't build on it—however zany—once it's been killed. Stretch your thinking; look at every idea as a springboard for creating a new approach by following the four steps we've just discussed.

The Magic of Flip Charts

I'm a big proponent of using flip charts during meetings. They are easy to use, and visual aids help sharpen your team's focus and encourage member participation. When all members are visually focused on the same content, their thinking is targeted and the words or graphics draw everyone into the process and energize them to stay on task. Effective public speakers use visual aids for the same reasons.

Some teams are initially reluctant to use flip charts, assuming that since each member is taking notes, flip-charting is just extra work that adds no value. The problem with having everyone keep separate notes is that the focus becomes individualized rather than collective.

While coaching a team that had this view, I decided to try to prove my point about the value of flip-charting. Their communication had become disconnected, participation was limited, and they were losing energy quickly. About forty-five minutes into their meeting, I asked members to share their individual notes with each other. When they read each other's notes, there were a lot of puzzled looks at first and then a burst of raucous laughter. One team member summed it up neatly when he said, "I think we've been attending different meetings together." They agreed to experiment with flip-charting and became quick converts once they saw how dramatically team focus and participation improved.

There is another major benefit of flip charts: you can tear them off the wall of your meeting room, roll them up, take them back to the office, and type them. They serve as full documentation of your meeting. Your minutes are done.

Flip-charting is not a lot of extra work and it's easy to do, once you get the hang of it. The person who captures the information on the flip chart is the recorder or scribe. If you've never stood in front of a room with Magic Marker in hand, you may see the role of scribe as a bit scary. I find that most people who feel anxious about being the scribe relax once they gain a better understanding of the role. The most important thing to understand is what it isn't. The scribe is not the moderator or facilitator of the meeting. As I've said before, although you may have one member playing the role of lead facilitator, all members facilitate the meeting since all members are responsible for the success of the meeting.

Your only responsibility as the scribe is to record the *content* of the meeting—the data the team is creating during the meeting and information the team intends to use in the future. Team members tell you what to write and you simply write. This can include ideas, plans, issues, decisions, and action items, to name a few. Spelling doesn't count nor does penmanship—though you should try to write fairly quickly and large enough for all to see. As the scribe, you are still a full participant in the team meeting, so continue to wear your thinking cap even while you are writing. Contribute to content just as you would if you were sitting around the team table, and don't forget to keep your eye on team dynamics.

One more helpful hint to scribes: use at least two different dark-colored Magic Markers on each chart. Creativity experts have shown that colors, in contrast to black and white, stimulate the right side of the brain and therefore enhance creativity and increase energy. Save your red Magic Marker for underlining or bulleting only. The color red can cause eyestrain and fatigue, and you don't want tired team members.

I encourage teams to rotate scribing responsibilities so that every member becomes comfortable in the role. It's a useful skill to have and one that you can employ in meetings other than your own team meetings. I know many people who were petrified when they first attempted scribing, and now they jump up to the flip chart every chance they get.

Meeting Minutes Made Easy

Have you noticed that a call for volunteers to do the meeting minutes is followed by what looks like a moment of prayer? All heads bow in total silence, eye contact is carefully avoided; then the one person who can no longer stand the silence groans out, "OK, I'll do them." No one relishes writing minutes. Most consider it a time-consuming, onerous chore. But minutes don't have to take hours and can be done quite easily, if you keep it simple.

Minutes are a recap of the content of your meeting. They are an important communication vehicle. They provide an update for team members who were absent from the meeting, they offer information to the rest of the organization, and most important, they help to clarify and confirm your decisions.

Constructing meeting minutes is a far less complicated task than we think. Let's look at a typical meeting. In terms of content, only a few things happen. Some members might have given status reports, surely we've discussed some topics, we've probably made some decisions, we may have taken assignments for action items, and if we're really organized, we've determined the agenda items, date, time, and location of our next meeting. So do we need a lot of prose? I don't think so.

The hang-up about writing minutes seems to be that people think they have to write a book or at least a chapter. Actually, if you've used flip charts to record your decisions and action items, and if team members have provided hard copy of their status reports, your minutes are just minutes away from typing. All you have to do is transfer informa-

MEETING MINUTES FORM

_____ MEETING MINUTES   Date:
(team name)   Attendees: _____

_____

_____

Status Reports: See Attached
Discussed: • _____

            • _____

            • _____

Decided: • _____

            • _____

            • _____

Action Items: Who   What   By When

            • _____

            • _____

            • _____

Next Meeting: Date:
                 Time:
                 Location:
                 Agenda Items:

---

tion from charts to computer, make copies of status reports, and distribute the minutes to all members within two days of the meeting.

Since the scribe has captured the pertinent information on flip charts, I suggest that he be responsible for writing and distributing the minutes. If you rotate scribing responsibilities, there's an added benefit. You'll no longer have to ask for volunteers; everyone will get a shot at doing the minutes.

Highlighting the information with bullets will provide the communication coverage you need and make the job a lot easier. Teams who have used the "Meeting Minutes Form" say it works nicely for them.

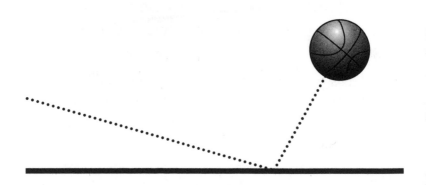

PART 5

Making Good Team Decisions and Putting Them into Play

Decisions, decisions, decisions! As a team you will be asked to make them, and if you are like most of the teams I've coached, you may be confused about which ones you are empowered to make. In fact, the whole concept of empowerment may be a mystery to you. The Notes in this Part will explain empowerment, provide advice on when to use specific decision-making processes, and offer techniques to make sure that you implement the decisions you make.

No Team Is Completely "Self-Directed"

Many organizations are steering clear of the term *self-directed* when describing their work teams. Instead they are using terms like *high involvement, high impact,* or *shared responsibility* as team descriptors. This is a good move.

The term *self-directed* has been misunderstood. It has created confusion, resentment, and chaos in many organizations—so much so that some organizations have disbanded their team-based structure.

The misunderstanding arises because words have different meanings for different people. Team members have taken *self-directed* to mean "We're on our own; we manage ourselves and our work; we make all the decisions with no intervention from management."

Management's interpretation is more figurative. They mean "We want our teams to share in the decision-making and problem-solving process; we want our employees to feel more empowered and involved in shaping not only the destiny of the organization but their own destiny as well; we want to take the concept of 'participative management' and notch it up a level to 'partnership management.'" Management's intention is to take a phrase from their annual report—"Our employees are our most valuable asset"—and make those words come alive.

The differences between management and employees concerning the meaning of the word *self-directed* has been costly and needs to be clarified for teams to operate effectively. Based on their interpretation, many teams have alienated themselves from management. I've heard teams say, "We don't want anyone from management to attend our meetings." Another common frustration voiced by team members is this: "Why should we invest all of our time and energy coming up with recommendations when management doesn't even look at them or ends up throwing them out the window? Let's just go back to the old way. Tell us what to do and we'll do it."

It's important to understand that no matter how well your team performs, you will never be totally self-directed. The hierarchy has changed, but there is still a chain of command. *Management wants you to make more decisions, but there will always be decisions that only management can make.* In fact, even your own management team is limited in its decision-making power.

No matter what the teams in your organization are called, if management's expectations are unclear, if you're not sure which decisions you can make and which decisions you can influence, ask. And keep the dialogue going; this is a dynamic, evolutionary process. Decisions that management can't share today may be yours to make tomorrow. The next Note discusses empowerment and offers some strategic tips on how to clarify decision-making boundaries.

It is equally important for management to understand that if it seeks a higher level of employee ownership and involvement, if it truly wants empowered teams, it must provide the right tools. And the right tools are information and knowledge about the business. As a team member you need to have an overview of what your firm does, not just knowledge of the function your team performs. You need answers to these questions: Who are our competitors? Who are our customers and what are they looking for now and in the future? What is our strategic direction? What constraints are we operating under? How are we doing in the marketplace? What does our financial picture look like? The more knowledgeable your team is, the more effective you can be as business partners.

How can you get this information if it's not forthcoming? This may sound somewhat simplistic, but the way you get it is to ask for it. Take charge—seek out the facts. Empower yourselves!

What Decisions Is Your Team Empowered to Make?

I was engaged in small talk with a friend during a cocktail party when out of the blue, she initiated some big talk. "Moe, I know you go around the country coaching teams. Are they as confused as I am about this whole empowerment thing? If I hear the word *empowerment* one more time, I'm going to get sick. The management at my company keeps saying 'We're committed to empowering our employees.' It sounds like it should be good for us, but no one understands what it is. And when we ask for an explanation, the answer we get sounds like gobbledygook. Maybe we're 'empowered' and we don't even know it. It's so exasperating."

Many teams have asked me the same question out of similar frustration. So what does empowerment mean?

Empowerment is the giving of power. To fully understand this notion of giving power, we need to define power. Power is the opportunity to influence an outcome or make a decision. Absolute power in an area is the authority to make all the decisions affecting that area. Some people have this kind of power because of the position they hold in the organization. Parents have this kind of power in the familial organization, teachers have it in the classroom, and managers have traditionally held this kind of power in the work organization. The manager of quality assurance, for example, is in control of specific functions related to the quality of the product. By virtue of his position, the organization pins a deputy star on his lapel authorizing him to make decisions concerning quality. He is fully empowered and in command. When he, in turn, authorizes others in his function to make some of these decisions, he relinquishes his power and gives it to them. They are now fully empowered to make those specific decisions.

There is another level of empowerment that we often overlook. Remember that power is the opportunity to influence an outcome: when someone asks for and listens to your opinion before making a decision, you are also empowered. Of course, the key words are "listen to." If the person doesn't listen to your opinion, there's no way you can influence her. Forget it; you're not empowered. She doesn't have to follow your advice necessarily, but for you to be empowered, she does have to consider it. There are two levels of empowerment then: you are fully empowered any time you have the authority to make the decision and partially empowered any time you have the opportunity to influence the decision.

So is your team empowered? Are you empowered? Maybe, as my friend Judy said, "You are, but you don't know it." Then again, maybe you're not. *The easiest way to find out is to identify who makes or influences the decisions for your team.* Take a look at the three decision-making modes described below. Then list the routine operational decisions—those made on a daily, weekly, or monthly basis—as well as the strategic decisions—those made in the last few months to correct a specific problem. Match each of the decisions to one of the decision-making modes.

Command decisions: Team members are given no opportunity to influence these decisions; therefore, you have no power in this decision-making mode. Quite often the power actually resides at a management level above your team leader and these decisions have been communicated to him. In these cases he is not empowered; he is simply relaying the message to you. Another possibility is that your team

USING A DECISION-MAKING SCREEN

To understand empowerment as it relates to your team, make it an
agenda item at your team meeting and follow these steps:

    1. Draw this decision-making screen on a flip chart.

A	B	C
COMMAND	CONSULT	TEAM
Management or team leader decides.	Management or team leader decides after considering input from one or two members of the team or from the entire team.	Team decides; team leader has influence equal to that of every other team member.

    2. Make a list of all the decisions made over the last three months
that have had a direct impact on your team or individual team members.
Include every decision you can remember: ongoing daily and weekly decisions, or more long-term strategic decisions.

    3. Reference your decision-making screen and identify the mode
that was used for each decision. Write an "A" next to each command

leader is fully empowered in this mode. He retains authority to decide
and then communicates both the decision and the rationale for the
decision to the team.

Consult decisions: Your leader makes the final decision, but before
doing so, asks for your input and takes it into consideration. You are
partially empowered in this mode because you have been given an
opportunity to influence the final decision. Once your leader decides, he
again communicates the decision along with the rationale to your team.

Team decisions: Your team or a team member makes the decision.
In cases where your team is making the decision, the leader may par-

decision, a "B" next to each consult decision, and a "C" next to each team decision.

4. How does your team decision-making screen look? As a team, discuss what you see. It's not a question of how many decisions fall into each box. It's whether the decisions are falling into the right boxes. Is the team leader or senior management making some command decisions that team members believe should be consult decisions because the team is closer to the situation? Are consult decisions being made that the team thinks they should make, for maximum efficiency? Is the team being asked to make team decisions which they feel ill prepared to make and which they think should be command or consult decisions?

5. The final step is to see if there is easy agreement among team members and between the team and management to shift certain decisions to a different mode. By *easy*, I mean that everyone wholeheartedly agrees that the mode currently being used to make a particular decision makes no sense at all and should be changed.

Using this decision-making screen will help you address specific issues. Rather than expressing a general discontent about not feeling empowered, you can pinpoint the decisions you see as falling into the wrong box.

---

ticipate in the decision-making process but his influence is the same as that of any other member. Your team is fully *empowered* in this mode.

Where do your decisions fall? If the command mode is being used for most or all of your decisions, your team is not empowered. Are there some decisions which you feel the team is ready to make and should be fully empowered to make? Tap the team mode. Are there some decisions that you feel you should, at least, be consulted on? Apply the consult mode.

The exhibit "Using a Decision-Making Screen" shows steps for understanding your team's decision-making modes. I use this process with many teams to explain empowerment and to resolve empowerment issues. One such case was a small legal firm that had recently decided that teaming was the way to go. They started by forming an administrative support team. Morale plummeted to rock bottom. Team members were complaining that, far from being empowered, they were being treated like third graders by, as they called them, "the ones doing the law."

The lawyers couldn't understand why the administrative support team felt this way. Using the decision screen showing command, consult, and team, I asked the team to identify who was making or influencing administrative decisions. It became very clear that their feelings were legitimate. Decisions about which supplies to order, when to call in the office machine repair service, how they would back each other up when a member was absent, how to arrange their working area, fell into the command mode. These were clearly decisions they were more than capable of making themselves. Additionally, management was considering refurbishing the office with new furniture, new equipment, carpeting, and so on, but without consulting the support staff. The team felt it should have input into these decisions.

When the attorneys saw the situation in black and white, they were shocked. They were honestly unaware that they had been making all these decisions. They not only understood why the administrative support team felt the way they did, but they also saw how inefficient it was for the lawyers to be involved at this level. Immediately they moved all these decisions to the *team* and *consult* levels. They have continued to use the decision screen as a discussion tool and have found it invaluable in placing decisions where they belong. Not only has morale improved, but the business is also running much more efficiently.

Decide How You Will Decide

Before you make a decision, give some thought to how you will make it. *How* you decide is just as important as *what* you decide. The process you use has a direct impact on how members feel about the decision. It can influence commitment, excitement, and buy-in; or it can create feelings of resentment and exclusion.

It scares me when teams tell me they use majority rule to make most of their decisions. For minor decisions this is fine. It's quick and easy and probably the way to go. For major decisions, however—those that require a high level of commitment to implement successfully or those that significantly affect team members' quality of life—majority rule can spell disaster. As the name implies, the majority does rule. They are the winners. They feel powerful because the decision went their way. But how does the minority feel? If you discussed the 1992 presidential election with any of your staunch Republican friends, you have a fairly accurate read. Because they had minimal influence, they feel powerless and are often disgruntled. No matter how good the decision, majority rule means that some people feel like winners and others feel like losers. The losers are generally not committed to carrying out the decision. And because they feel excluded, they often subconsciously (and sometimes consciously) sabotage the team's efforts. You may have made a great decision, but because all members are not on board, implementation may be shaky at best. When you need commitment, ownership, and smooth implementation, use the consensus process. It's time-consuming and sometimes frustrating, but in the long run it's well worth the effort.

Let's take a look at the consensus decision-making process. Many people misunderstand it. For starters, if you have unanimous agreement you obviously have consensus, but unanimous agreement is not necessary for consensus. The Merriam-Webster Dictionary defines consensus as "a collective opinion." I take it a step further. My team dictionary says consensus is "a collective agreement among team members to support a decision actively." In other words, team members don't have to be of one mind about the decision. Some members may disagree with the decision, but if they agree to give it their full support, you have reached consensus.

Most likely you've heard the expression "building consensus"— and building support for the decision is what takes so much time. I worked with a team of eight members who were planning to reorganize their workload—clearly a major team decision. After some discussion, one member suggested that rather than have one member responsible for mail distribution, they rotate this responsibility on a regularly scheduled basis. Six members voiced their approval; two members, Julie and Eric, were vehemently opposed. Here's where the building begins. Both the majority and the minority share responsibility for building support for the final decision. The majority must make a concerted effort to understand the concerns of the minority. In this case, the six members refrained from pushing their idea, invited Julie and Eric to express their objections, listened attentively, and in general demonstrated a willingness to be influenced.

Having been given sufficient air time, the minority now has the responsibility of working with the majority and, for the good of the team, finding some way to provide active support to the ultimate decision. Often, all that is required is a slight tweaking of the original idea. Sometimes, an entirely original suggestion comes out of the discussion.

There are also times when the majority shifts its thinking completely and sides with the minority view.

In this situation, Eric, who was in the minority, was anxious about making a change. The mail had been one of his major responsibilities for over two years. He had developed a system that worked and he was comfortable with the task. "I don't have the technical skills the rest of you have. What am I going to be doing if I'm not distributing the mail?" As the team listened, they began to realize that Eric felt his job was at risk. It didn't take long for the team to identify other ways Eric could contribute. These functions would require minimal training, expand his knowledge base, and make him an even more valuable asset to the team. Although he still disagreed with the decision, he agreed to support it actively.

Julie was also concerned about taking partial responsibility for the mail, but for different reasons. She was heading up a high-visibility project and was under a great deal of pressure. She indicated that once the project was completed she could share in distributing mail, but until then it was too much of a burden. The team understood her feelings and agreed to delay her participation. The team reached consensus: all members vowed to make the change work. You can imagine what might have happened had the team used majority rule to make this decision.

When in doubt about whether you're dealing with a major or minor decision, try this: ask your teammates for a show of hands. "Raise your hand if it makes a big difference to you whether we decide to go this way or that way." If you see some raised hands, you are more than likely dealing with a major team decision. Take the time and use consensus. If no hands go up, you probably have a minor decision. It makes no sense to spend a lot of time discussing the options in this case. Majority rule will work.

Brainstorming: Use It at the Right Time

Teams seem to be addicted to brainstorming. I coached a marketing research team that used brainstorming just about every time they needed to make a decision. I was afraid to ask members when they wanted to break for lunch for fear they'd want to brainstorm a list of possible times before deciding. They started to work on establishing their goals for the following year and once again said, "Let's start by brainstorming." I had been trying to understand this recent phenomenon, so I blew my whistle.

"Why do you want to brainstorm again? What's behind your preference for brainstorming?"

"It's a great way to get started," one member said. Others chimed in, "Everybody is involved. We all feel safe because, at least in the beginning, nobody critiques your idea. Every idea is listed on the flip chart— no questions asked. I think that's why our energy level is so high."

The last member to speak said, "Lots of times I don't think we're quite sure how to get started. When we feel stuck like this, brainstorming gets us off the dime. It gives us the feeling that we're making progress."

Their reasons for using brainstorming didn't surprise me; unfortunately, they are all the *wrong* reasons for using this wonderful technique. Brainstorming is great when you're looking for creative solutions to a problem or for innovative approaches for seizing an opportunity. It's intended to stimulate right-brain activity, to help you look at things differently. It encourages you to color outside the lines, to diverge from your logical line of thinking, to forget the traditional paradigms. When used in *these* situations, brainstorming can be valuable.

But the situation is different when you're facing a problem or making a decision for which you have all the information and which requires a hard look at the facts. In this case, creativity is not what you need; a rational, left-brained approach is much more effective. Opting for a brainstorming approach in these cases might, in fact, mean that you're simply delaying making a decision. At these times, it is far more appropriate to engage in some dialogue. What ever happened to this very natural form of communication? Dialogue is a decision-making technique that can be just as spontaneous as brainstorming, but it allows you to comment on and debate ideas as they are brought up and helps you do what brainstorming does not: make a swift decision.

It is not that dialoguing is better than brainstorming; they are both great techniques, but they serve different needs. It is important for you to use the method that best fits each situation. As I asked my research marketing team, "Do you need to be imaginative to come up with your team goals?"

The answer was "No, we pretty much know what we need to do." They started a dialogue, and much to their surprise, even after a slow start, they liked it and were very good at it.

Of course, using a dialogue is not the only problem-solving and decision-making technique available to you. Force field analysis, fish boning, root cause analysis, and priority gridding are only a few of the other approaches that work very well when you need to make a decision based on the facts at hand. Mind-mapping and story-boarding are methods similar to brainstorming, designed to get your creative juices flowing. A number of books have been written on these techniques and there are many excellent consultants who conduct focused workshops on problem solving and decision making. Treat yourselves to some training in this area. Learn how to use these techniques and, perhaps most important, when to use them.

Do Great Minds Really Think Alike?

If your team members have a lot in common, you probably get along well together and your communication is easy. Because you see things much the same way, your relationships are solid and your work as a team is free of hitches. You may even think you're the perfect team. Don't be fooled by the ease of it. Thinking you are the perfect team may be stopping you from becoming a great team.

I was misled by just such a "picture perfect" team recently. It was a team of six white women, all in their mid-thirties and all human resource professionals, humming along beautifully—productivity and cohesiveness in motion. Quick to agree with and support each other's ideas, they made team decisions with amazing speed. I thought, "My God, what am I doing here? They really don't need any coaching. I should put them on video and show the world a high-performing team in action."

When I pointed this out to them, one team member said, "We do seem to think alike. You know what they say: great minds run in the same channel."

As I continued to observe their dynamics, I sensed that something was missing. When I found myself dozing off, I knew what it was: team energy, excitement, and creativity. I began to wonder if their speedy decisions were the best decisions they could make. My experience with other effective teams was so different. Those teams were composed of people with different personalities and diverse backgrounds. I had seen them debate, question each other, struggle, stretch their thinking, and build on each other's ideas. They created solutions and made decisions that no one individual on the team would ever have thought of.

I shared my thinking with this homogeneous team of great minds and asked them to humor me awhile. My suggestion was to have one member of the team play the role of devil's advocate. Before the team finalized a decision, this member was to ask questions such as these: Is this just a Band-Aid solution or are we really solving the problem? Have we thought of all our constituents? Is this the way we've always done it? Could we do something different and make it better?

They were about to close discussion on the design of a new employee recognition program when the devil's advocate spoke up. "We've created what looks like a dynamite program but I'm concerned about the increased cost and I'm not really sure it's going to work. What we're trying to do is improve employee morale and I feel the real issue here is not the award itself but how it is presented. That's what our employees are complaining about. We need to figure out how to get management on board so they will use the program and use it right."

Their final design ended up costing less than their existing program and from what I've heard from employees, is very successful.

At first, they were visibly uncomfortable with the new process. The notion of debate didn't fit into their norm of peaceful and civil discussion. However, once they realized that their decisions were of higher quality than they had attained previously, as difficult as it was for them, they embraced the process.

If you are a team with many similarities in terms of age, sex, values, and background, you may have to work just a little harder to be a great team. Don't think that because you are all quick to agree, you are making the best decisions. Before you close on a decision as a team, you might try asking, "Have we stretched our thinking enough? Have we jumped to our conclusions too quickly? Is this really the best we can do?"

My experience with teams says, "Great minds run in very different channels. When those minds manage their collective diversity, the result is greatness."

Who's Got the Ball?

One of Ross Perot's campaign one-liners really struck home with me. He repeatedly said, "Just because you talked about it, don't think you did it." My variation on that theme, directed toward teams is, "Just because you decided to do it, don't think you did it."

Last spring, I asked a group of team members if they had established their team goals for the year. One person piped up, "We're way ahead of you, Coach. We did that quite a while ago—way back in December of last year."

"That's great," I said, "How are you doing with implementing them?"

A long pause followed. Then another member asked the team, "Wait a minute—what goals are we talking about? Do you mean that list we put together when we went off site to that conference center?"

As it turned out, that was indeed the list. Everyone remembered having decided on that list of goals, but no one could remember specifically what was on it. One member volunteered to bring the list in the following day. He was pretty sure he knew where he had filed it.

This is a true story about one team. Unfortunately, it's not uncommon. Teams often make decisions and then neglect to implement them. If you make a point of planning the action steps immediately following your decision, you'll be more likely to follow through on implementation. Many teams have adopted this practice as one of their ground rules. As soon as they decide to do something, they ask, "*What* are the next steps? *What* do we need to do to make this happen?" These end up being the action items. The next question is, "*Who's* got the ball on each of these actions?" Each action item now has a member's name assigned to it. That person is responsible for making sure it happens.

The last question is vitally important and is directed to each member who has agreed to complete an action item: *When* will you have it done? Now each action item has a deadline date attached to it. There's a lot to be said for that. When we establish a completion date for something we plan to do, we are much more likely to do it. It also helps to include these action items in your meeting minutes as a reminder to everyone who signed on.

To ensure clarity, many teams take the process a step further. The scribe wraps up the meeting by summarizing all the decisions the team has made along with the action items the members have committed to.

It's very simple. Answer these three questions and your decision is now out of the file drawer and into the "do it" basket: What needs to be done? Who will do it? When will it be completed? If you take the time to plan what you have to do to win, determine who's got the ball, and when he or she is going to shoot, you are more likely to score.

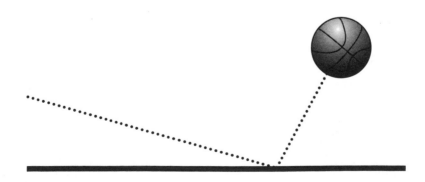

PART 6

Notes for Team Leaders

It is not enough to say that your company is making the shift to a team-based organization; management needs to commit to the change and demonstrate its commitment through action and example. Even the best team will get stuck if they do not have the support of their team leader and their organization's management.

The seven Notes in this Part speak directly to senior management and team leaders about the pivotal role they play in creating an organizational climate where teams can flourish. It is written to the team leaders and management, but I encourage team members to read it as well. Only when team members and management have clear and accurate expectations about each other's roles, decision-making boundaries, and responsibilities will an organization have successful, high-performing teams.

Why Teams Get Stuck

Often I'm asked by senior management, "What can we do, as the leaders of the business to ensure that our new team-based structure will be successful?"

I reply, "Try to keep your teams from getting stuck. Any team can get stuck. A team that has everything going for it will fail if the environment is not conducive to teaming."

I've had many exciting assignments over my fifteen years of coaching teams, but none compares to the challenge of working with teams that are stuck. I use the term *stuck* because that's how they describe themselves—that's how they feel. The way they tell it, there are forces working against them. Sometimes they know what the obstacles are but feel there is little they can do to overcome them. Other times they can't even identify the obstacles and feel very much out of control. My challenge as head coach is to unravel the mystery and find out what is blocking the team.

After many years of experience, I now know where to start my search—and it's not with the team itself. Teams don't generally get stuck because of something they're doing or not doing; they get stuck because they have some critical needs that are not being met. I immediately home in on the environment and I always suggest that senior management does the same to learn whether the following five essential team needs are being satisfied.

Teams need support and nurturing from senior management. As a senior manager, you play a pivotal role in making good things happen for your teams. It's just not enough to talk teaming; you must also "walk the talk." That means walking into the locker room, visiting the team, and asking, "How are things going? How can we help you win this game? What resources do you need? Is there some information that would be helpful? What's getting in the way? Are there some obstacles we can remove?" Then it means taking action on those things you say you will do and following up with the team to see if what you did helped.

Offering your support means sharing the strategic direction you have in mind. I can't tell you how many teams are confused or don't have an inkling about their organization's strategy. A candid admission that "we're really not sure, but here's what we're going to try," is infinitely better than no message at all. Another way to demonstrate your support is to break out the champagne when the team has been victorious. Recognizing the team's achievements can give the members a tremendous lift.

When sports teams play at home they talk about having the "home court advantage." That's because their fans are there cheering them on. Business teams are no different. Check out the Note in this Part, "Invest in Your Team's Self-Concept," to further understand a team's need for cheerleaders.

Teams need stability. When teams have to adjust to constant change in membership and leadership, they never get grounded and therefore don't get a chance to stabilize. They are always regrouping—going back to the forming stage where they have to sort out role definitions and responsibilities. You can put together the most talented players available, but if they don't have the opportunity to get to know each other's moves, they may all look good individually but collectively they look and feel awkward. Watch any all-star professional sports event and you'll see what I mean. It's just not the same as watching a well-oiled team whose members have played together year after year. Teams can adapt to an ever-changing work world when they feel rooted in their own identity.

Teams need some power. When members feel they have little to say about who will do the work or how the work will be done, they tend to do one of two things: they either crawl back into their individual shells and operate on automatic pilot, or they engage in power plays, trying to usurp the little influence each one has. And when teams are unsure of the decision-making boundaries, team members tend to get frustrated, throw up their hands, and say "Fine, we're just playing the same old game; just tell me what to do and I'll do it." Teaming is supposed to be a new way of life in the organization. If team members' expectations about decision making don't even come close to management's, that "stuck" feeling comes on pretty quickly. See how one organization aligned these decision-making expectations in "Name That Decision" later in this Part.

Teams need time. Many organizations expect teams to be up and running and productive overnight. Unfortunately, that's just not the way it works. In fact, during the forming stage of a team's life, it's not unusual to see a slight drop in productivity. I've seen teams get stuck during this stage simply because they aren't given the time to do the developmental tasks they need to do. Just when they need time to establish team goals, define team roles, organize the work flow, and structure their meetings, they get bombarded with additional responsibilities, special projects, shortened deadlines, and sometimes reprimands for poor performance. Between a rock and a hard place, they attempt to do it all—form the team and meet the new requirements placed on them.

They end up falling short on both and feeling stuck.

Teams need influential leaders. A leaderless team will almost always get stuck, and a team with a leader in name only usually doesn't fare much better. In filling "team leader" positions, many organizations make the mistake of naming one of the members of the team as the leader, with the thought of rotating the position every year. The team in this situation has two chances of succeeding—slim and none. It's the blind leading the blind. The problem here is that this so-called leader has no more positional power than any other member and, therefore, has minimal opportunity to influence more senior people in the organization to obtain the resources, direction, information, and support the team needs. Read more about this need in "Every Team Needs a Leader with Clout."

Every Team Needs a Leader with Clout

If you are managing an organization and are considering a transition to a team-based environment, please keep this advice foremost in your mind: every team needs a leader with clout. The early stages of a team's development are particularly crucial. I've seen many groups attempt to become a team and never make it through the forming stage, simply because they lacked direction. Then I've seen others who have made it through the forming stage but who became so frustrated with the dysfunctional dynamics that naturally accompany the storming stage that they just gave up and disbanded. And when teams don't disband voluntarily, management often decides that teaming doesn't work and chooses to revert to the old structure. Every time I've witnessed this scenario, it's been because the team did not have a leader with *positional power* or because the *team was leaderless.*

A teaming environment is not a democracy. When an organization changes its structure to a team-based design, the shift does not mean that reporting relationships are erased. Teams should report to someone and for the good of the team, that someone should have clout in the organization.

It is ludicrous to assume that a team can succeed without a leader. That is analogous to saying to a young child, "I'm sure you'll figure this business of life out; you'll be able to get what you need; you don't really need a parent" or expecting a professional sports team to win the championship title without a coach to monitor their performance and give them feedback. The leader plays a pivotal role—as parent during the forming stage as he or she helps the team to create its identity, and as coach during the storming stage as he or she facilitates the team's learning process. And throughout all stages, the team leader is very much the educator. Team members eventually emerge as leaders and they begin to learn how to share leadership, but that doesn't happen until the norming stage of their development. Even during that stage and through the performing stage, the team needs a leader, although the team leader is not as critical to their progress. During these stages, the team leader's most important function is to serve as the champion of the team.

Don't leave your teams in the lurch to try to figure teaming out for themselves. Give them the resources they need, the most important of which is a leader with clout.

Name That Decision

Team leaders have told me that this tip—"Name That Decision"—
has been invaluable. If you know in advance that you and you alone
will make a particular decision—that it is not up for team discussion—let your team know that. They will appreciate your candor. I've
seen teams invest a tremendous amount of time discussing a problem,
even going so far as deciding how to resolve it, only to discover that the
decision was never theirs to make. It was a command decision that the
leader had intended to make all along. You can imagine how frustrating this is for a team. They've not only wasted their time, but worse than
that, they feel that their value has been diminished. This pattern had
become so much the norm for one team that they balked at working
out problems at all. Their attitude was, "Why bother? Our team leader
will let us know what he's going to do anyway." Teams generally understand that they are not empowered to make all decisions. It makes their
work a whole lot easier, however, if they know when they are empowered and when they are not.

Actually, any time you can clarify the decision-making boundaries
in advance, you will be doing yourself and your team a big favor. The
clearer you can be about who will be making the decision, the less confusion and frustration you will cause for the team. If you're going to
make the final decision but want to get the team's perspective first, let
them know that you're using the consult mode. Be sure to listen and
confirm your understanding of their ideas. One additional caveat here:
don't fake the consult mode. If you've already made up your mind, you
have made a command decision. There's nothing that destroys a team's

morale more than a leader who asks for its opinion when she has already made her decision.

If it's a team decision—one that team members are fully empowered to make—let them know that too. Be sure they understand that your opinions relative to the decision carry no more weight than theirs and that whatever the team decides is what will be done.

Who will make which decisions is an ongoing, continuous question for teams and team leaders. Wouldn't a team's life be easy if the answer could be etched in stone? It would also become boring quickly. The inferred message would be, "These are the decisions you can make now and forever," a condition that automatically negates the team's potential for learning and development. There are decisions that the team may not be capable of making today simply because members don't have the business acumen, technological expertise, relevant information, or general experience dealing with particular problems. But if you are fulfilling your role responsibilities as team leader, you are providing them the opportunities to develop the skills they need to take on added decision-making responsibility. In fact, a sure sign that a team is developing into a high-performance team is when command decisions become consult decisions and consult decisions become team decisions. Keep the team posted as they grow through the decision levels.

I shared this tip with the senior management of one of my client organizations, which was about to launch its team-based design. They applied it in a most impressive manner. As part of their kickoff, the head of the organization presented decision-making guidelines. She listed all the decisions she could think of under three headings: decisions that management and team leaders will make, decisions that team leaders and management will make after consulting with teams, and decisions that teams are fully expected and authorized to make. She stressed the point, ensuring that the teams understood, that these guidelines were just a starting point. Some command decisions, she said, would always be management's to make, such as policy and strategy decisions; but decision-making authority would evolve as teams were ready to take on added responsibility. With the decision-making boundaries clarified, the teams were off to a great start.

Invest in Your Team's Self-Concept

I have a friend who is obviously short and chubby, yet when she looks in the mirror she sees a tall, slender lady. Her positive view of self carries over to everything she does in life. She exudes confidence, doesn't think twice about trying something she's never done before, and succeeds in all her endeavors. Another friend always looks like she just walked off the cover of *Vogue;* she is strikingly beautiful. But she suffers from such a negative self-concept that all she sees in the mirror are skin blemishes, ten pounds of excess weight, and hair that never looks right. Although quite capable, she is unwilling to take risks and is never satisfied with the results of her efforts. One of her favorite lines is, "Even as a kid, when I'd finish one of those paint-by-number pictures, you could never tell what it was supposed to be."

The power of the self-concept is extraordinary! How do these self-mirrors form? Why does one person feel so good about herself and another feel so insignificant and incapable? I'm not a psychologist but I am convinced that a lack of positive feedback and an abundance of negative feedback will always result in a negative self-concept.

Just like a person, a team has a self-concept. This is a story about five teams I coached in one organization about nine months ago. All of them suffered from a negative self-concept. It was very sad. Even though each of these teams had achieved many of its goals, members felt worthless. They worked hard to do whatever was asked of them but initiated nothing on their own. None of the team members was having any fun, nor were they terribly excited about their accomplishments.

When I first started working with them, it was obvious that they could benefit from some team building. I spent two days coaching each team and was encouraged with their adeptness in picking up the skills. At the same time I was discouraged because I sensed that they wouldn't really apply what they were learning. No matter how many times I told them they were doing well, they didn't believe it. They had their own mirror and it was an extremely negative one.

No one in the organization nurtured or supported these teams. There was nobody at the finish line cheering them on. Each of the teams had a designated facilitator—not a leader. The facilitators were supposedly there if the teams needed them, but none of them was a team champion with—as the teams said—"skin in the game." The facilitator entered the picture only when things were going poorly. So what did they get? Lots of negative feedback. I discussed this problem with the president of the organization and offered specific suggestions about how she could remedy the situation. It was a self-concept problem: the teams needed some cheerleading, some positive reinforcement when they did things well. They needed a leader who was invested in the well-being of the team—someone who cared about how they were feeling as well as how they were doing.

My diagnosis was confirmed a few weeks ago. I received a phone call from the human resource manager requesting more coaching for the teams. This is not unusual—in fact, I encourage follow-up coaching for all teams six to eight months after our initial session. When I asked how the teams were doing in general, he said, "Not well at all. They don't seem to be using any of the skills they learned. Morale is very low and their productivity is way off." The president of the organization had distanced herself even further from the teams and the teams were still leaderless.

I did not take the assignment. I explained once again that these teams needed a new mirror and the only way they were going to get it was with a big dose of support, encouragement, and positive feedback from management.

Yesterday I came across a poem hanging in a golf pro's office. In talking with his staff who had presented it to him, they explained that the poem described him to a tee (no pun intended). Having met him I heartily agree. The poem is titled "The Man Who Thinks He Can," by Walter D. Wintle (Felleman, p. 310). I have changed the title to "The Team Who Thinks It Can," modified the text accordingly, and forwarded it to the president along with this memo: "Your teams do not need training. They *can* do it. They just have to *believe they can.* Your role and the responsibility of your staff is to form a cheerleading squad. Get in the game before it's too late."

The Team Who Thinks It Can

If you think you are beaten, you are;
If you think you dare not, you don't;
If you'd like to win, but think you can't,
It's almost a cinch you won't.
If you think you'll lose, you're lost,
For out in the world we find
Success begins with a team's will;
It's all in the state of mind.

If you think you're outclassed, you are;
You've got to think high to rise.
You've got to hustle before

You can ever win a prize.
Life's battles don't always go
To the stronger or faster team;
But soon or late, the team that wins
Is the one who thinks it can.

From Manager to Team Leader

A very wise friend once gave me a priceless piece of advice: "Whenever you're not sure of your role in a given situation, ask the people with whom you'll be working what they expect of you. Then negotiate from there. If you can meet their expectations, fine. If you can't, tell them what you can and cannot do." I tested this advice on my first assignment as an internal management training consultant and it worked.

I've coached many managers who have taken on new assignments as team leaders. They know this new role should be different from the manager's role they've played in the past, but they're not quite sure how. If you find yourself in this situation, I suggest you take my friend's advice. Ask your team members what they expect of you. And as part of the negotiation process, let the team know what you expect of them.

The more expectations your team can articulate, the better the discussion will go. I have found that you get many more ideas if you break the team up into smaller subgroups with each developing an expectations list. Provide a general framework by suggesting any or all of the following "complete the sentence" list titles: "We expect you to . . . ," "We feel you are responsible for . . . ," "We'd like to see you behave in these ways: . . . ," "You could really help us if you would/would not . . ." In the meantime, develop two lists of your own. Entitle your first list "I feel I am responsible for . . ." and your second list "I expect the team to . . ."

When the team gets back together, have all the subgroups present their lists. Ask them to elaborate and give examples as much as possible rather than just reading their list. Do the same with your lists. Then start the negotiating process and see whether you can come to a meeting of the minds.

I remember facilitating this process for a new leader of a components assembly team. Her team said, "You could really help us if you would stop constantly looking over our shoulders to see if we're getting the work done. When you monitor our performance so closely it makes us feel like you don't trust us." It is interesting that one of the items on her list was, "I expect the team to inform me early on whenever they think we won't make our production numbers." This was a perfect match in expectations. She agreed that as long as the team would warn her of any performance slippage, she would not monitor so tightly.

This process is a great starting point for gaining clarity about your new role. However, your team's needs and expectations will constantly change as they grow in and out of their developmental stages. It makes sense then to review expectations continuously.

How Successful Team Leaders View Their Role

How do you view your role as team leader? It's an important question for you to think about. I ask it because I'm convinced that how you see your role directly influences your leadership behavior. For example, if in your mind, the team leader is the person in charge of getting the work done, you may tend to dictate how the work is to be accomplished and who will do it. In other words, you'll come across as the boss. If you see the team leader as the person responsible for developing teamwork skills among members, you will look for opportunities to educate and act more as the coach.

I posed this question recently to two folks who had successfully moved from manager to team leader. Here's what they had to say. I couldn't describe the team leader's role any better.

The first team leader saw many similarities in this role and that of being a parent:

> If there's anything that can prepare you for this role, it's being a parent. It's not that the team members are babies or immature; it's that your job is to help give birth to a team and then bring it from infancy to a high-performing stage. Every day you must answer this question: "What's happening for the team right now and what do they need?" During the forming stage, teams need more direction, structure, and guidance. They need to be clear about management's expectations and understand how their performance will be measured. Then once the team takes on its identity and members begin to bond with each other, they need support, encouragement, and confidence build-

ing. And every team needs continuous education. So the team leader's role, like the parenting role, is really a combination of many roles.

The other team leader stressed the coaching role, articulating the difficulties and rewards of no longer being completely in charge:

> One of the hardest things you have to do is let go and give up control. You're not the boss and even though you're still a part of management, your job is not to manage the team, it's to lead the team. I see myself as the team coach. My major focus is to prepare the team to take on new tasks and develop their team interaction and decision-making skills. Once they're ready, I must be willing to let them do their thing. Your ultimate goal is to have a team that is able to manage their own operations. Once the team members are sharing leadership and can collectively lead the team with minimal dependence on you as the designated leader, you've achieved your goal. You're really trying to work yourself out of a job. This notion is a little scary at first, but once the team can take care of business on the operational side, you actually end up with more time to devote to strategic issues.

In the next Note, "How Winning Teams Describe Their Leaders," you'll get a sampling of how these same two leaders behave. I think you'll agree that their leadership behaviors very closely match their perceptions of the team leader role.

How Winning Teams Describe Their Leaders

After hearing how two successful team leaders perceived their roles, I asked each of their teams this question: "What specific things has your team leader done to contribute to your team's success?" Their responses so aptly describe effective leadership behavior that I often use them as discussion tools for new team leaders. In describing what their leaders do, the teams indicated the different roles the leaders play:

Motivator:

"We have a motivator in our leader. She reminds me of my high school hockey coach. She praises us when we've done well but then she's always getting us to look at how we can do it even better."

Nurturer:

"We've had our share of disasters on this team but somehow our leader has helped us get through each one of them. We never feel like we'll be left out there hanging on the edge. She senses when we're down on ourselves and helps us get out of our funk. She's very supportive; actually, nurturing is probably a better description."

Coach:

"When we are struggling with a problem, our leader doesn't tell us what to do. He'll offer his advice and suggest that we consider certain things, but he lets us solve it. But if we really get stuck, we can count on him."

Public Relations Agent:

"Our leader always gives us credit when we perform exceptionally well. She makes sure everyone knows about our successes. It's almost like having our own public relations staff. She also gives us opportunities to make management and customer presentations, which gives us great visibility. It used to be that only our manager made those presentations. It sure makes us feel good."

Demonstrator of Trust:

"Our leader doesn't come across as the boss. I feel like he trusts us—nothing like our prior manager who would tell us what to do, when to do it, how to do it, and then breathe down our backs while we did it. Don't get me wrong; our leader is crystal clear about what we need to achieve, but then he gets out of the way and lets us do it."

Developer:

"We've reached the high-performing stage so we hardly see our leader any more. She checks in with us every so often and we know she's there if we need her. We're doing most of what she used to do and we're making many of the decisions she used to make, so now she's off working on some special projects."

Observer:

"Our team meetings are very effective and we owe that to our team leader. He showed us how we could facilitate ourselves. Every once in a while we slip and engage in some dysfunctional dynamic and then he'll point it out but otherwise we conduct our own meetings."

Cheerleader:

"Our leader is one huge cheerleading squad. She's a 'you can do it' person and is constantly encouraging us to take calculated risks. It's great working with her because you know you can try something new and if it doesn't work, there's no penalty."

Counselor:

"In the beginning, our leader worked very closely with us. We didn't know what teaming was all about. He really helped clear up the confusion. He explained the steps we needed to take to become a team and then helped us write our vision statement, identify our team goals, and establish our ground rules. We would have floundered without him."

"Thanks to our leader, we know more about the business than we ever did before. It seems like information that used to be for management's eyes only is now ours to see. It makes a big difference being in the know like this. We feel like we're an integral part of the business."

Teacher:

"Our leader is an educator. She has turned our team into a living case study. Her favorite question is 'What can we learn from this?' No matter what goes wrong, once we fix it we figure out how to prevent it in the future."

Mediator:

"When we can't resolve our conflicts, our leader serves as a mediator. He encourages us to try to work out the problems for ourselves, which is good, but he doesn't want any conflict left to fester. He is a great listener and has a knack for helping us come to resolution."

Champion:

"We tell our leader what we need or what obstacles are in our way and he always goes to bat for us. A few members needed technical training and all of us needed team training and he arranged it for us. We can count on him."

If I asked members of your team to describe your leadership style, how might they respond? The best way to find out is to ask them. I encourage all my team leaders to ask their teams for feedback periodically. Don't expect your members to be as complimentary as these members were—after all, I only asked them for the positives. If your feedback is half this glowing, I'd say you're certainly on the right track. The wonderful part about getting feedback is that you will know what you're doing right and how you can improve.

If your team is in the forming or storming stage when trust levels tend to be low, you might start the feedback process by asking each member to respond anonymously to these two questions in writing:

1. What specific things am I doing that seem to be helping the team?
2. If you were the team leader, what would you do differently?

After you've had a chance to read the responses, be sure to follow up with a discussion at a team meeting. If the team is in the norming or performing stage, there's probably no need for members to respond in writing. Just put "team feedback to the leader" on the agenda and ask members to respond verbally to the same two questions. Just a reminder—don't forget to ask team members to follow the steps I've outlined in Part Three on how to give feedback constructively, and do make sure to follow the steps for receiving feedback.

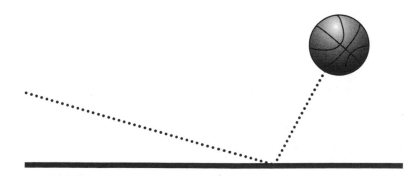

A Letter from the Coach

Dear Team:

Someone once said, "If you want to get letters from your friends, write letters to them." That's why I'm writing to you. I am starving for fun, interesting mail. I don't know about you, but bills just don't do it for me. I want to go to my mailbox every day and see bundles of letters addressed to "Coach Maureen O'Brien." I want very much to hear from you.

As your coach, I need some feedback (mind you, only the constructive kind!). I'd like to know how you applied some of the tips I've discussed and which points were particularly helpful. I'm also interested in learning about other nagging questions you may have about team life that were not covered in this book. And of course, I'd like to hear about any winning plays you've developed that have helped you to succeed.

It has been a pleasure coaching you throughout these pages. Like all dedicated coaches, I want to continue coaching you and learning from you. Write me and I promise to write back. If you need additional advice for a particular situation that is blocking your progress, I will respond with some suggestions. All teams need continuous coaching and I am here to do that for you.

In the meantime, get in the game (be committed), put on your game face (stay focused), aim before you fire (have a game plan), keep asking, "Who's got the ball?" (implement your decisions), and by all means, have fun (celebrate your victories).

Looking forward to hearing from you.

Sincerely,

Coach Maureen O'Brien

Coach Maureen O'Brien
P.O. Box 20038
Myrtle Beach, SC 29577

References

Alter, J., Michael, R., and Lerner, M. "America's Q&A Man," *Newsweek,* June 15, 1987, pp. 50–56.

Felleman, H. (ed.). *Poems That Live Forever.* New York: Doubleday, 1965.

Keidel, R. W., and Associates. *Game Plans: Sports Strategies for Business.* Wyncote, Pa.: Dutton, 1985.

King, P. "What It Takes to Win." *The New Haven Register,* Aug. 6, 1993, p. 5.

"Teamwork and Empowerment on the Rise." *The Quality Digest,* Nov. 1993, p. 10.

Tuckman, Bruce W. "Developmental Sequence in Small Groups." *Psychological Bulletin,* 1965, *63,* (6), 334–399.

Wagner, Jane. *The Search for Signs of Intelligent Life in the Universe.* New York: HarperCollins, 1990.